KINGDOM GOVERNMENT

Kingdom Secrets to Restoring Nations Back to God.

ABRAHAM JOHN

Kingdom Government

Kingdom Secrets to Restoring Nations Back to God

Copyright © 2017 by Abraham John

Published by Abraham John
Maximum Impact Ministries
www.TheKingdomNetwork.org
Email: Info@TheKingdomnetwork.org
Phone: 1 800 588 5020

ISBN: 978-1-948330-54-1

Printed in the United States of America

CONTENTS

Preface

*"The crown has fallen from our head.
Woe to us, for we have sinned!"* – Lamentations 5:16

As I write this, I am sitting in my hotel room in Dar es Salaam, the capital city of Tanzania. My room faces the main bus terminal, where people from all over come to catch buses to travel to different provinces. Through the window, I can see the bus terminal and the streets filled with people. The city comes to life before dawn. People are hurrying to get to work and kids are going to school early. They are all trying to survive, trying to make a living. This country is at the top of the lists for witchcraft and sorcery.

I can sense in my spirit the whole city is under a bubble of religious witchcraft. Creativity and vigor of life has been stolen from them and life has been reduced to a mundane task where they wake up and do the same thing every day. People don't know why they are here, why they are alive, or who made them. They are not living the life God wants them to live. They are part of the system created by the kingdom of darkness, a system that slowly draws human beings into total destruction.

During that trip, I also had the privilege to visit the world-famous wildlife habitat Maasai Mara in Kenya. It was one of the most amazing sites I have ever seen. I saw wild animals in their natural habitat. Previously, I had seen them only in zoos and circuses.

I saw lions, giraffes, elephants, hippos, and other animals living their lives to the fullest. I didn't see any animal sitting down worried about their food or their tomorrow. They are all free and full. They eat, play, and sleep. We had to leave our room early to go to the wild to see the animals, especially if we wanted to see the lions. Our driver said the lions come out early in the morning to hunt their prey and don't like to be in the hot sun. They eat and go into the bushes to lie down in the shadow. That is very interesting to me.

The Bible says the animals of the field ask God for their food and He feeds them all (Psalm 104:20–21, 27–28). Not one goes hungry. The animals we saw the most were the wildebeest. That's what they call them. We saw thousands and thousands of them all over the fields, grazing and moving along as a group. Then we saw something strange (it was the season when the wildebeest migrate to Tanzania). We saw what seemed to be an unending line of animals. It looked like the Israelites coming out of Egypt! They were all going in a line to cross the border to Tanzania. I could only see the back end of the line.

There is an abundant supply of food in the wild for all these animals. None of them looked skinny or hungry. The only animals we saw that were skinny and hungry were the cows the Maasai people were taking care of.

I read online that more than twenty thousand children die in Africa every day because of hunger or hunger-related causes. In all the earth, the only part of creation that lives in hunger are human beings—the very people who are created in God's image and likeness.

The very people to whom He gave dominion over the earth. I don't think as many animals die on that continent because of hunger. Why do so many humans live in hunger?

Humans are supposed to live in God's kingdom and they cannot thrive without it. In every city you see the same picture: People are busy and there are always those that comb through garbage piles looking for plastics and other materials they can collect and sell to make a few pennies to fill their stomachs.

The rich think they are living a better life than the poor. They ride around in cars and go to work in an office or for a company. They spend their lives and energy in the pursuit of one thing: Money. Is that all there is to life on this earth?

Who is living a better life, the rich or the poor? The rich think they have an advantage over the poor because they have better conveniences, but the bottom line is they are all working for the same thing, money. They are not serving God and they are not fulfilling their purpose.

That is why Jesus said we cannot serve two masters. Who are the two masters? They are God and mammon (the god of money). Most people don't realize this because they have been brainwashed and programmed by the Babylonian system.

In the East, people are poor and you can see it. In the West, people think they are rich because they have *things*—but they do not own them. They get to use them as long as they make payments on them. The banks own most of the land and houses. It is another form of poverty, but people do not realize it.

We need to create alternative economies and communities that do not depend on the world system and not live in deception. Who are the losers in the end: Those who waste their one lifetime on things that don't matter at all. By the time they realize the truth it is too late.

What is worse than realizing that you have lived a lie all your life and never recognized it? The majority of people on this planet are living a lie, deceived by the religious spirit or by the spirit of mammon.

When Jesus sent His disciples to heal the sick and cast out demons, He specifically told them to tell the people the kingdom of God is at hand (Matthew 10:7; Luke 10:9). Today there is little focus on the kingdom. Preachers and believers are afraid to talk about it fearing they would be called a heretic.

There is plenty of food and other resources on this earth for every human being that is alive. Why then are they not reaching those who need it the most? A very small percentage of the landmass of this planet is inhabited. There is plenty of land for everyone and no need for anyone to be homeless or living in hunger. All of the wealth God created is still here; no one has taken anything out of this earth. It only changes hands and locations.

The reason we are not reaching people is the lack of proper governance. We have governments that are working against everything God intended for them. They pass laws that are against human conscience and natural laws. Then they wonder why life is not 'working' as it should.

Jesus never told any other creature to seek His kingdom. He only told that to humans. All other creatures are happily living and fulfilling their purpose. Instead of seeking His kingdom, we have been waiting for the end to come. He said that if we seek His kingdom, all the things we need in life will be added to us.

When the End Will Come

When we preach the gospel *of the kingdom* as a witness to all the world, in all the nations, then the end will come (Matthew 24:14). Now the question is: the end of what? What is the end? When it says "end," it means the end of this age, the present age. How will it look when this present age comes to an end?

Throughout the Bible, we see the end of many ages. Age means a particular way God dealt with this earth and the human race. When Adam was kicked out of the garden, one age came to an end. When God gave the law to Moses, it was the beginning of a new age. That age ended with John the Baptist, and a new age began. How did the Old Testament age end and a new age begin? He implemented a new system, an operating system. He introduced His kingdom to His people.

That age is going to come to an end and another will begin, but God is waiting for us to finish the task He gave us. When we complete that assignment the next age will begin. How will this new age look? It will be the rule and reign of Christ on earth (Revelation 11:15).

We are on the brink of this new season. Many think they are waiting for God but He is waiting for us. May this book help to open our eyes to see our world as God sees it and to do what we are supposed to be doing.

"But this Man, after He had offered one sacrifice for sins forever, sat down at the right hand of God, from that time waiting till His enemies are made His footstool" (Hebrews 10:12-13).

Introduction

"If the foundations are destroyed,
what can the righteous do?" – Psalm 11:3

The church is supposed to be on the forefront of innovation, leadership, and development in every nation on earth. That is what Jesus meant when He said we are the light of this world and salt of the earth. We are supposed to be the pioneers and sustainers of this planet but something tragic happened to the church over the past few centuries. We are supposed to be *conceiving* from the Lord in the wombs of our spirits what He wants to do on earth, and release it to the physical realm for the benefit of humanity. Unfortunately, the church is more than a few years behind in everything that is happening in this world. We have been trying to catch up with the world when instead; the world should try to catch up with us!

When we stop being innovative and creative we become irrelevant to the society we live in. When we stop learning we stop growing and become unproductive. God never stops expanding or innovating. As long as He is in existence He is doing something new, and there will be something new to learn about Him. When we fail to provide leadership and innovation in the arenas of life the enemy takes the opportunity and fills that vacuum with his agenda.

Most believers walk around like neutered creatures that have lost touch with the reality of what is happening in their nation. They have a pie-in-the-sky mentality and are waiting to escape the earth instead of making an impact for God and His kingdom right where they live.

We blame the wicked for being wicked and doing the wickedness they were born to do. It is the same as blaming a dog for barking. How does that help the dog or anyone else? Dogs are created to bark. The reason we blame everyone else for our problems is because we do not know what we are created to do and feel dissatisfied and unfulfilled in our hearts.

Think with me for a minute. What if the whole world were to come into the church today and become like us? What would happen to this world? Have you ever thought about it? What if they think and act like us? We wouldn't have the majority of the products we use today, and most of humanity would die of starvation because there wouldn't be enough food production. The church is the most consuming agency on earth and does not produce much.

There wouldn't be very many to rule in government and we would be a hundred (or more) years behind in development and innovation. Everyone would be walking around looking for another conference or goose-bump experience. Do you think that is what God wants to happen on this earth? We have been telling the world for a long time to become like us. Thank God He is not answering our prayers!

The Jewish population, for example, has influence. I never saw a Jewish worship team go into cities and countries giving concerts.

But, I notice Jewish people at the top of every sphere of society. They are in government, business, science, the arts, and all noteworthy positions in society. They represent less than 0.2 percent of the world population, but they also represent more than 10 percent of the Forbes 400 list of the world's wealthiest people, more than 10 percent of the Fortune list of the CEOs of the 500 largest corporations in the world, and almost 30 percent of Nobel Prize winners in several categories. Why? How did they reach those positions without worshiping God like the church and without the long preaching we have?

Many so-called Christian music groups have been visiting Israel and conducting concerts on the Temple Mount and other various locations, trying to teach Jewish people how to sing like we do. We think they are not spiritual enough and not fulfilling their purpose because they are not worshiping as we do. Lord, have mercy! We are trying to convert them to become singers like the church and to have the same escapist mentality. I hope and pray that the Jewish people will resist and won't buy into the nonsense we've been trying to put on them. In the same way, I hope and pray the church won't buy into the religious nonsense that some Messianic Jewish groups have been trying for a very long time to put on the church.

Jewish people believe in their hearts that God made them to be the head in every nation. They know they are supposed to be above and not beneath. They not only believe it, but they work hard to make it happen. Though the church received the same promise through Jesus Christ, we have been acting like orphans for too long. One problem with the church is that we have been waiting for God to do everything we should have been doing all along. Every promise God gave to Israel is applicable to us through Christ Jesus. Without keeping the ceremonial laws and requirements, we get to enjoy the same covenantal blessings.

The *church* taught me that I was created to worship God. Almost every Sunday morning while I was growing up I heard from the pulpit that God created man to worship Him. Without ever questioning what I was hearing, I believed it because it came from the church pulpit where the *man of God* was anointed to bring the oracles of God straight from the throne room of heaven.

I believed that lie for many years. When things became difficult in my life and ministry and I was not receiving any result from the worship/singing I was doing, I decided to check the Bible to see where God said in His Word that He created me to worship Him. I went to the book of Genesis to see what God said to Adam when He created him.

I could not find a single word in Genesis where God asked Adam or anyone else to worship Him. That startled me. It was difficult to accept the fact that I had believed a lie for such a long time. My spiritual pride combined with absolute ignorance had kept me in the dark for a very long time.

I saw the *light* for the very first time. Though I was a Christian and had been in ministry for years, I was living a lie taught by the religious spirit. I encourage my fellow sojourners to check out for yourself everything you hear from the pulpit, in the light of the Scriptures. If it is not in His Word, and if it is not applicable to us, I would strongly encourage you to throw it out and never look that direction again.

If God did not create me to worship Him, then why did He create man? I believe Genesis 1:26 is the first verse from the Bible that every new believer should memorize. In that single verse, God Almighty explains in detail the very purpose for which He created the human race. Unfortunately, it is only the so-called church that does not know its purpose. For some reason, Muslims, Hindus, Jews, the birds, the fish, and every other group out there knows why God created them and put them on earth. I wonder who told them about their purpose? The stupid devil has a better understanding about the purpose of our life on earth than most believers.

Many believers will pick a fight the moment you tell them God created them to have dominion over the earth. They will come up with all kinds of excuses and reasons to talk themselves out of it. The religious spirit has done a great job of causing them to believe the lies of the enemy. It is almost impossible to teach anything new to a person whom that spirit blinds.

The church also taught me that when I die I will go to heaven and sing and worship Jesus for thousands and thousands of years. If the first thing the church taught me was wrong, I decided I'd better check this out as well. I went to the Bible to find where it says that man will sing in heaven for thousands of years. Not only could I not find any reference to man singing in heaven, I could not find a single reference to humans doing anything in heaven at all, at any time! That shook and rattled my faith and theology altogether. If I won't be singing in heaven, then what will I be doing there for all eternity? Playing foot ball?

I found that the Bible says the same thing about man's purpose in the book of Revelation as it does in the book of Genesis. God is not the author of confusion. He is not schizophrenic, as some people seem to think. He does not say one thing today and something different tomorrow. He is the trust worthiest Person in the whole universe. In fact, He is the *only* completely trustworthy Person. Nothing and no one can change His Word because it is forever settled in heaven.

Throughout the Bible God says the same thing about man's purpose: We are created to rule and reign on this earth. The earth is our permanent and eternal home. This may be shocking news for some of you readers. Please read the following references and then make the decision for yourself. Don't believe anything just because I said it, but research the Bible and find out what God says about you. You are responsible for your own life and decisions.

> "Then God said, 'Let Us make man in Our image, according to Our likeness; let them have dominion over the fish of the sea, over the birds of the air, and over the cattle, over all the earth and over every creeping thing that creeps on the earth'" (Genesis 1:26).

> "The righteous shall inherit the land, and dwell in it forever" (Psalm 37:29).

> "Blessed *are* the meek, for they shall inherit the earth" (Matthew 5:5).

> "There shall be no night there: They need no lamp nor light of the sun, for the Lord God gives them light. And they shall reign forever and ever" (Revelation 22:5).

As I searched the Bible I found something else very interesting. I found out who is singing in heaven and what they are singing. Most of the time they are singing about the earth and what is happening here. In Isaiah 6 we are given a glimpse into heaven. Isaiah had a powerful revelation of the Lord sitting on His throne high and lifted up. Seraphim were singing and worshiping Him.

> "Holy, holy, holy *is* the Lord of hosts; the whole earth *is* full of His glory!" (Isaiah 6:3).

They were singing *to* the Lord and *about* the earth. I wondered why God cared so much about this earth to fill it with His glory if He is going to burn and destroy it. God is more concerned about this earth than we know and understand.

In Revelation 5:7–10 we see another glimpse of what is happening in heaven and what they are singing about. I found that it is the twenty-four elders and four living creatures singing in heaven. Let's look at what they are singing about.

> "Now when He had taken the scroll, the four living creatures and the twenty-four elders fell down before the Lamb, each having a harp, and golden bowls full of incense, which are the prayers of the saints. And they sang a new song, saying:
>
> 'You are worthy to take the scroll,
> And to open its seals;
> For You were slain,
> And have redeemed us to God by Your blood
> Out of every tribe and tongue and people and nation,
> And have made us kings and priests to our God;
> And we shall reign on the earth.' "

They are singing about man reigning on the earth. Have you ever heard a single song by any Christian artist during your lifetime about us reigning on this earth? I haven't. But I have heard several songs about us flying away and singing in heaven for thousands of years. I could not believe that I had lived a lie for all those years, and I discovered why my life was not going anywhere. The foundation of my life and faith had been laid wrong.

It is time for us to catch God's vision for our lives. Many of the songs we sing in church need to be thrown into the trash because they are a mockery to God and His Word. When you sing something opposite to what God says and call it worship it is dangerous - even if it is done in ignorance.

As a result of believing those lies, any time I tried to build something it came crashing down and I had to begin again from scratch. I had to root out, pull down, destroy, and throw down the old religious stuff before I could build anything new. Most believers start a new life every Sunday morning or in a conference. They go from Sunday to Sunday, from conference to conference instead of from glory to glory, and their spiritual depth is only good enough to sustain them for a few hours.

I had to throw most of my theology (that which I inherited from my church) into the trash because it was not based on the Scriptures. It sounded more like fables or folk stories that had been passed down from one generation to the next. No one took the time to stop and think about why they were doing what they were doing. We just kept on parroting what others were saying, when all along we knew in our hearts there was something wrong and things were not working the way they should have worked. But no one knew why. We all believed that someday things would get better; now many years have passed and we are still waiting.

Then I heard the famous slogan of evangelism: to *plunder hell and populate heaven*. I spent a few years of my life trying to help God populate heaven, though I could not find any verse to support God asking us to populate heaven. Jesus did not tell His disciples to go and plunder hell and populate heaven. He told them to go into all the world, and to disciple nations.

I found plenty of Scriptures that said we were created to populate the earth, so I had to throw that out as well. It was never man's assignment to plunder hell and populate heaven. God did not create man to populate heaven; man was created to populate the earth. God has no lack of creatures in heaven and He never wanted His children there; He wants His children to rule the planet earth for Him.

Those are all slogans people came up with because of religious zeal, but they were not based on true knowledge of the Word of God. Heaven is not in need of anything from humans. It is self-sufficient because it is the kingdom of the Lord God Almighty. He won't ask a human to help Him with anything in heaven. He is El Shaddai, the All-Sufficient One.

What God is doing in this age and time is this: Restore man to his original intent and purpose. Unless man is restored to his original purpose, nothing can be fixed on earth. That is what God is doing right now. He is not trying to send revivals, shaking, or dancing; in fact, He is tired of our singing and shaking with nothing to show for it or present to Him.

From all the above verses we draw the conclusion that man's eternal purpose is to reign on the earth forever. Whether it is this earth or the new earth our purpose will not change. Every person God used in the Bible reigned over something. They were either rulers of nations or over different systems of nations. We have a religious mentality that has us believe that we have to wait until the millennial reign of Christ to rule and reign on earth. There are no scriptures to support such beliefs. From the beginning until the end and for all eternity, man was created by God to rule and reign on the earth. I want that to settle deep in your heart and spirit, rooting out every religious belief system you had until now. Every time those old religious beliefs try to spring back up, take dominion over those thoughts.

The Pentecostal movement reached the whole earth, and you will see churches all over the world as a result. But the Pentecostal movement was not complete. People were saved and filled with the Holy Spirit, but there was too much focus on speaking in tongues. As long as someone speaks in tongues, they are happy. They will train people to the level of speaking in tongues and stop growing because they think that if a person speaks in tongues, they have arrived! That's a huge misconception.

We are supposed to be growing to the fullness of Christ. Salvation is the beginning of life with Christ and speaking in tongues is the beginning of life with the Holy Spirit. They are not the destination: They are entry levels. Christ is the door to His kingdom, and speaking in tongues is the entry level to everything the Holy Spirit is and what He knows. He is the Spirit of wisdom, knowledge, and understanding. The Holy Spirit is much bigger than His gifts.

God sent the Pentecostal movement to restore the gifts of the Holy Spirit to the body of Christ. He sent many other movements, like the Jesus movement, the holiness movement, the faith, healing, and prosperity movements, etc. They were all intended to restore something the church had lost. Because of the deception of the religious spirit, people get stuck in different movements and begin to specialize in that particular truth and take it to an extreme. Instead of uniting the body of Christ, these religious extremists created divisions and denominations. Now, at the end of this age, He is sending the kingdom movement to restore everything we lost since Adam walked on this earth, and to unite the body of Christ worldwide.

Jesus said that many would come at the end and say to Him, "Lord, we cast out demons, healed the sick, and did many wonders in Your name." He will tell them He never knew them because they were the workers of iniquity and lawlessness (Matthew 7:21–23). Why would Jesus call those who cast out demons and healed the sick in His name "lawless ones"? If casting out demons, doing wonders, and prophesying in His name are not His will, then what is His will in this day and age? It is because they were not following the law of God, the laws of His kingdom. I thought everyone who calls Him Lord will be saved.

Go Back to the Roots

Any time I meet someone from any country, they complain about how bad the government in their nation is and speak negatively about their leaders. This will not change anything for the better. The only way to bring change is if we have witnesses for Jesus in those governments. We need believers in positions of influence, striving for kingdom causes. We must find out why we do not have any influence in government and come up with a solution.

One popular message of the last few years has been to tell America to go back to its roots. That message is dying out. America cannot go back to its roots by just preaching about it. We need a new strategy.

There were fifty-six men who signed the Declaration of Independence. Out of those fifty-six, *all* of them were known to be Christians and attended some form of church.[1] That means their moral and ethical value systems were based on biblical ethics. That is why this country was established the way it was. How many people do we have in our government now with those ethics? If we are going to take this country back to its roots, we need believers in positions of government—at the local, state, and national levels—who will witness Jesus as the King. This is beginning to happen.

We are not here to take over governments, but like Joseph and Daniel, we need to have people with influence in high places. Believers should be presidents, prime ministers, and governors. In fact, it is necessary. That is the purpose of this book. Every single person God has ever used manifested Christ and His mission on earth through their own life. We have received the real deal, and today there are fewer witnesses for Jesus than ever in world governments.

---

1 "Religious Affiliation of the Signers of the Declaration of Independence." Posted July 4, 2010. *Free Republic*. http://www.freerepublic.com/focus/news/2546951/posts/. Accessed February 15, 2017.

To do this, we need to train kings to be in positions of government and execute God's purpose in their regions. To know more about kings and their responsibilities, please read the book, *Releasing Kings and Queens to Their Original Intent*. You can order it at www.kingdomawareness.org.

Before reading this book, I recommend that you read the other volumes in the Kingdom Awareness Series. You can find them at www.maximpact.org. Then only will you have a complete picture of what God is trying to communicate through me in this book.

PART I

Understanding Politics and Government

Chapter 1

Government – Something Very Close to God's Heart

I would like to share with you something that is very close to the heart of God. We are entering into a new season, a season that we have never seen or experienced before. The body of Christ is going through a shift. More believers and preachers are beginning to talk about government and as never before. That excites me and that excites God!

Neither God the Father nor Jesus is a religious leader. They are political leaders or Kings. When we talk against government or politics we are talking against what is close to the heart of God. There is not a book in the Bible that does not talk about government or politics. So you can feel safe now, knowing that I am not going to talk about anything weird or that is not scriptural.

The Bible is not a religious book. It was not written to a particular religion or with the intent of starting one. The entire Bible is about a King, His kingdom, His governing body, His royal family, and His will and plan for planet earth. It was written to help us live on the earth effectively and accomplish the will of our King, right here. It is not a book about how to go to heaven or how life works in heaven.

Whatever God does, He does through governments. Without government He will not do a thing. Believe me on this. Read your Bible once again and examine each incident that happened and the connection it had to the government of that time. Even the birth and death of Jesus was orchestrated through the government. The reason for Joseph and Mary to come to Bethlehem was the rulers of that day ordered everyone to go back to their hometown for a census. And, you know who was instrumental in crucifying Jesus, Pilate, who was a political leader.

Sixty-six books in the Bible talk about government and politics. When I heard that from the Holy Spirit I was shocked. I asked God about books like Titus and Philemon? He said that Philemon is the most political book in the entire Bible! I was taught in Bible school that those letters are pastoral letters. Paul did not write those letters addressing pastors. Please show me in the titles of those books where Paul says he was writing those letters to pastors or to Pastor so and so. No, that is not the way those books begin. Timothy and Titus were part of his apostolic team.

Why has the church stayed away from government and politics for so long? There are three reasons. First, we were deceived by the religious spirit, which tells us that politics and government belong to the devil and his kingdom. Second, we were just ignorant about it: No one taught us about government and politics. And, third, we did not know it was close to the heart of God.

Still, even though many of us believed that politics is bad and that government belongs to the devil, almost every believer and minister that I know talks about it. Why? I will tell you why. Because of wrong teaching and programming in our head we thought they are bad, but our heart knows it is something we need to be a part of. So we have this love/hate relationship. With the heart we love it but with the religious head we hate it.

I will tell you why we are interested in talking about government and politics. We are created as kings, rulers. What do rulers and kings talk about normally? Kingdoms right? Your spirit was formed in a way that it is natural for you to show interest in politics and government. It will be against your very nature when you talk against it. You are sinning against yourself. Please don't do that.

Repent and please do not continue to do that. Instead, try to learn as much as you can and you will see your spirit man becoming excited. You were created to rule. If everything you do is against that, you are deceived and cheating yourself out of the very thing God created you for.

When I was in High School, I wanted to major in politics but my father rebuked me and said no. He said I needed to study science or biology because he wanted me to become a medical doctor. So, according to him it was ok to be in the world and in the profession of a doctor but not a politician. He was a staunch Pentecostal by the way.

In the United States, the enemy divided the church and state and kicked the church out of politics. Practically, the government told the church, "We do not want you here. You go to your church buildings, sing songs every Sunday morning, preach cute sermons, and help some of the poor if you can, and we will take care of the rest." That was the biggest mistake in US history. But it is changing now. More preachers and believers are beginning to talk about politics and government as never before.

If government and politics are very close to the heart of God, how did we miss it for so long? We missed it because of the deception of the religious spirit. What is the shift that is happening in the body of Christ now? We are finally getting a glimpse of what Jesus wanted us to do from the beginning.

We have been so focused on evangelism, as if Jesus told us to go and evangelize the whole world. He did not say that. In Matthew 28 He told us to go and make disciples of all nations. We thought He meant go and evangelize nations. That is not what He said. Please open your Bible and read it for yourself.

We also thought He said go, meaning travel, around the whole world and preach the gospel to humans. He did not say that either. In Mark 16 He told us to go *into* the whole world and preach the gospel to all creatures. Please read that also. Those are very important commandments. We have been going *around* the world for so long, we never went *into* the world.

The shift that is happening is this, we are entering into a season of transitioning from *evangelizing* the nations to *discipling* nations, and from going *around* the world to going *into* the world. From a religious church to a kingdom Ekklesia. From all other types of evangelism to kingdom evangelism. From preaching the gospel of salvation to preaching the gospel of the kingdom. From the church age to the kingdom age. Unless we go into the world we cannot disciple nations.

Jesus knew that as soon as He left this planet His disciples were going to cry to get out of this world. Jesus is very smart. So He prayed a powerful prayer in John 17. In verse 15 He said (paraphrased) *Father, do not take them out of this world. I know they are going to cry and ask you to get them out of here when things are tough, but I am praying now, in advance, that you will not listen to their cry and take them out of here. Keep them here because this is where I want them the most.* That is very interesting!

There is only one place in this entire universe that God has any need of us. That is right here, on this planet earth and in this world. Not in heaven. If God wanted all of us in heaven He would have kept us there from the beginning. He would not have sent His only Son to die for us. He did that because He cares for this planet and the people who live on it.

Jesus never said, "I am the way to heaven." No, He said, "I am the way to the Father." Those are two different meanings. Everyone needs a father. There are no perfect fathers on earth because the majority of people carry a father wound. So He said, I have to come show you the way to the only perfect Father. He also said that He is the door to the sheepfold. Not heaven.

This is why we have stayed away from politics for so long, because we did not understand what politics means. Most people, when they think of politics, think of different political parties and what they stand for, and their views on important issues of life. What an unbeliever thinks of life and a believer in Christ thinks of life, is totally different. We cannot expect an unbeliever to believe and uphold the same values that we uphold and believe.

What is Politics?

Politics is a combination of three Greek words. The first is *Polis* meaning city, as in Indianapolis, meaning the city of Indiana. There was a place in the New Testament called Decapolis, which was a group of ten cities. The next word is *politas,* meaning citizen. And, the third word is *politikos, which* means the affairs of the sate or citizens. From those three words came the word we know today called politics.

Politics simply means the science of government or the process of governing. In the Bible days there was only one form of government, kingdoms. Most nations were ruled by kings. There are different types, or forms, of political processes or systems. When kingdoms began to disappear because most kings became evil and unrighteous, man came up with other forms of government, other than kingdoms. It took hundreds of years to establish the different forms of government and political processes we see today.

When a believer, or a minister, says they are not interested in politics, they are actually saying they are not interested in the affairs of their state or the citizens of their country. What kind of ignorance or deception is that? In their right mind, no believer will say they are not interested in the condition of their city or other citizens. That is the whole purpose of us being here as people of faith.

Communism, socialism, and then finally democracy, are simply different types of political processes to form a government to manage the affairs of its citizens.

According to the definitions mentioned above, you now know why I said the book of Philemon is the most political book in the entire Bible. Philemon is a book that was written about a slave who ran away from his master and was put in prison. While he was in prison, he happened to be in the same prison cell as Paul. Paul shared the gospel with him and he was saved.

The Apostle Paul wrote to Philemon, his friend, telling him to receive his slave again, because he repented and became a child of God. That is politics, dealing with the affairs of the citizens, or people. That is the most political book that I can think of maybe next to the book of Esther.

The time has come for the body of Christ to become what Jesus meant for us to be from the very beginning. He never wanted His body to be a music group. He always wanted us to be a political or governing body. May the Lord help us to make that transition fast and peacefully. May our eyes be opened to see life here on earth as He sees it. May He use this book to do that in Jesus' mighty name, Amen.

Chapter 2

Kingdom Government

*"Of the increase of His government and peace
there will be no end"* – Isaiah 9:7a

As I said, in every nation I visit, I hear the same news: People are not happy with their government and the politicians who are in authority. Wherever I go I also hear more sad news: Believers are not happy with the current church and they are leaving in droves. Is there a solution to these dilemmas we are faced with in our societies? I believe there is. This book will offer you clear-cut scriptural solutions to both problems mentioned above.

Our God is a King and He has a kingdom.

As the body of Christ, we are supposed to be witnessing Jesus as a King. He is not just a king, but also the King of kings. He is the only person who is a King eternal.

Every nation has a government, and many nations are facing the problem of failed government. People are tired of their governments, and they are complaining about the leaders and their corruption. What is the solution? The solution is to raise up a new generation of people who will witness Jesus as a King. What do kings do? They govern.

"The Lord *is* **King** forever and ever" (Psalm 10:16a; 29:10b).

"For the kingdom *is* the Lord's, and He rules over the nations" (Psalm 22:28).

"For God *is* the **King** of all the earth; sing praises with understanding" (Psalm 47:2, 7).

"Your kingdom *is* an everlasting kingdom, and Your dominion *endures* throughout all generations" (Psalm 145:13).

He is also called the King of glory.[2]

"Where is He who has been born **King** of the Jews? For we have seen His star in the East and have come to worship Him" (Matthew 2:2).

"Now to the **King** eternal, immortal, invisible, to God who alone is wise, *be* honor and glory forever and ever. Amen" (1 Timothy 1:17).

It is the nature of a king to expand his rule, territory, and culture to new frontiers. Kings are always looking to extend, conquer, and establish their kingdoms in new places. Man has the same nature because we are created in that image and likeness. We are always looking for new horizons to conquer and new mountains to climb, continually pushing the limits of everything we know.

---

2 See Psalm 24:8.

It is in the heart of every man to build, create, establish, govern, manage, and rule. When a man is not able to do that, he gets frustrated. God created woman to be by the side of the man to help him do that. When a woman is not doing that, she feels frustrated and out of place.

Our God decided to expand His kingdom, so He created a planet called Earth. He needed someone to manage or govern it for Him. He couldn't come and live on the earth because the earth is a physical planet and those that operate on this planet require a physical body. It is also the nature of a king that when they conquer or establish a new territory, they appoint either their children or a close associate to rule and manage it.

In this case, God decided to create a species called humans in His own image and likeness—with the same qualities He has—and to call them His children. He filled them with His own Spirit so they could relate with Him on His level and think and act the same way He does.

God created everything He wanted on earth and then finally, He created and put the man in charge of it all (Psalm 8:3–9; 104:24). God had an enemy on Earth because this planet was his kingdom prior to the creation man. Because he messed up his assignment and misused his authority, the King removed him from his position and destroyed his kingdom on the earth with a flood that we see in Genesis 1:2. For some reason, God did not remove the enemy from the earth, so he waited on the earth for an opportune time to strike back. Please read the book *Releasing Kings and Queens to their Original Intent* to know more about this.

The King deposited an enormous amount of His kingdom wealth and resources on this earth for man to use to establish His rule. He brought all the animals to man to see what he would call them.

Whatever man called them became their name. Man was managing the earth for his King.

God told man to have dominion over everything He created. *Dominion* means to subdue and rule. That is man's purpose. Every human being is created with the instinct to rule over something; Everything God created rules over something. That's the way His kingdom operates; all forms of creation represent Him and reveal an aspect of His nature and glory.

> "You have made him [man] to have dominion over
> the works of Your hands;
> You have put all *things* under his feet,
> All sheep and oxen—
> Even the beasts of the field,
> The birds of the air,
> And the fish of the sea
> That pass through the paths of the seas"
> (Psalm 8:6–8).

God never mentioned anything about going to heaven, or singing, to Adam. He was created as an eternal spirit being and put into a physical body. He was not created to die. Death came because of sin because the wages of sin is death. He was supposed to be fruitful, multiply and fill the earth and rule it forever and ever. That was and still is man's assignment from the Creator. God never changed His mind about man's purpose or what he is supposed to be doing.

The Bible says the heavens belong to God and the earth He gave to the children of men (Psalm 115:16). Instead of taking care of what He gave us, we have been coveting His property for a long time: desiring to go to heaven.

What if Adam hadn't disobeyed God and fallen? What would his children be doing now on this earth? They would be ruling, right? That's exactly what we are supposed to be doing. Jesus came to restore and redeem what Adam lost and what the devil stole from us. Once it has been restored, we are supposed to do what God originally commanded Adam. That is what salvation is all about. If you are saved from sin, you go back to your original assignment.

It is impossible to govern earth properly without the help of heaven. When we exclude God from any type of government, it will eventually fail. God designed government in such a way that it will work only when we include Him. The reason is that all authority comes from Him.

Throughout human history, man has tried to come up with different types of government and make it work without God. Communism, socialism, and the like all failed miserably, and, at last, democracy and capitalism are also on the brink of failure. Is there a solution? The solution is *Kingdom Government*: governments that function as extensions and instruments of God's kingdom on earth.

Attempting to impose a certain type of government upon a group of people who are not ready for such a government forces those people into a state of anarchy or civil unrest. Every nation on earth is not at the same level. They are all at different stages of development and maturity. All humans mature in stages, and so do nations.

It is a misconception to think that every nation is ready for a democratic government. Recent history proves otherwise. When the United States went to the Middle East and removed totalitarian rulers and then tried to introduce democratic elections, it didn't go well with the nation or the people. There is unrest while they try to learn and cope with the new system.

One good thing about the democratic form of government is that an ordinary person with the right skill and ability can aspire to the highest office in a nation. In a kingdom, or in a totalitarian government, that is never possible.

It is God's plan and purpose for His will to be done on earth as it is in heaven. That's why He appointed and allowed governments to be formed. In the beginning, He created the garden of Eden and appointed Adam to govern. That was the first government on earth. Ever since man disobeyed and we lost the kingdom and the government, God has been trying to reestablish His government on earth.

That is why Jesus never mentioned anything new to His disciples. He repeated what God did and told Adam in Genesis. Everything else He said was the process of how to get back to what He intended for us in Genesis. The only difference was that He showed by example how to rule and reign. He taught and demonstrated to them in real life how to have dominion. The chart below shows the similarities.

Genesis Chapters 1–3	New Testament
God created man in His image and likeness (Genesis 1:26)	When we are born again, we are recreated in the image and likeness of God (John 3:3 and Colossians 3:10)
God blessed them and told them to be fruitful (Genesis 1:28)	Jesus blessed us and told us to bear fruit (Matthew 5:3–9 and John 15:16)
God told man to subdue the earth and take dominion over every creature He had made (Genesis 1:28)	Jesus told us to tread on serpents and scorpions and over all the power of the enemy (Luke 10:19)

Genesis Chapters 1–3	New Testament
God gave Adam the earth as his inheritance	Jesus said the meek shall inherit the earth (Matthew 5:5)
God put man in His kingdom, the garden	Jesus came to restore and give us the kingdom (Luke 12:32 and 22:29)
There was no sickness or curse in the garden	Jesus came to die for our sickness and curse and gave us authority over all manner of sickness and disease (Matthew 8:16 and 10:1)
God breathed into man His Spirit (Genesis 2:7)	Jesus breathed His Spirit on the disciples (John 20:22)
God gave them His Word (Genesis 2:16–17)	Jesus gave us His Word (John 17:8)
They were clothed with God's glory (Genesis 2:25)	Jesus said that He gave us His glory (John 17:22)
God instituted marriage (Genesis 2:22–24)	When Jesus referred to marriage, He referred to the original marriage (Matthew 19:4, 8)
God walked with man (Genesis 3:8)	Jesus walked with us and dwelt among us (John 1:14)
Adam had unlimited knowledge and wisdom (Genesis 2:19–20)	Jesus possesses the treasures of all wisdom and knowledge, and He lives inside of us (Colossians 2:3)

Genesis Chapters 1–3	New Testament
Man had dominion over the earth (Genesis 1:26)	Jesus said all authority in heaven and on earth was given to Him. In turn, He gave that authority to us. He said that whatever we loose (permit) on earth will be loosed (permitted) in heaven; and whatever we bind (forbid) on earth will be bound (forbidden) in heaven (Matthew 16:19 and Ephesians 1:22)
God told Adam everything in the garden was freely his	Jesus said, "Freely you have received, freely give" (Matthew 10:8, Romans 8:32, and 1 Corinthians 2:12)
God gave Adam a woman	The church is pictured as a woman
Adam was the son of God (Luke 3:38)	Whoever believes in Jesus becomes a child of God (John 1:12)
Genesis starts with "In the beginning" (Genesis 1:1)	The gospel of John starts with "In the beginning" (John 1:1)
God's will was done on earth as it was in heaven. There was no curse, sickness, poverty, or death in the garden.	Jesus taught us to pray the same (Matthew 6:10)

Genesis Chapters 1–3	New Testament
God did not ask Adam and Eve to sing to Him	Jesus never asked anyone to sing to Him
A river came out of Eden, parted into the four corners of the earth (Genesis 2:10–14)	Jesus said the rivers of living water will flow out of us to the uttermost parts of the earth (John 7:38; Acts 1:8)
God told them to multiply and fill the earth (Genesis 1:28)	Jesus said to go and make disciples of all nations (Matthew 28:19)

We don't have the history of how Adam lived before the fall, what he did, or how he functioned. To fill that gap, God sent another Adam (the Bible calls Him the last Adam) to show us how to live on this earth as humans. If we study the life of Jesus, we get an idea of how humans are supposed to live on earth.

The first thing Jesus taught His disciples was not how to heal the sick and cast out demons. The first thing He taught them was how to exercise the law of dominion when He helped them catch fish in Luke 5. When they discovered the law of dominion they left their boats and businesses and followed Him. They were inspired to follow Him not because they saw the material blessings He had but the life of freedom and authority He lived.

When God created Adam, where did Adam's blood come from? Not from the mud. It came from God, right? From where did his DNA come from? From God, right? Adam had the blood and DNA of God. Whether God has blood or not, I am not sure. But I am trying to say that Adam's blood was from God because he didn't come from another man, He came from God. Man had the same essence of God in Him. The Bible calls Adam a son of God (Luke 3:38).

If we have the same DNA of God, we are supposed to be acting and doing things like God does; but because of the programming of the religious spirit over hundreds of years, we have lost touch with the God-part of our lives. We became mere creatures living lower than we are supposed to live. In many parts of the world, animals are considered more valuable than humans. In India, men kill humans and worship cows. If you kill a cow, the Hindus will kill you. In other parts of the world, dogs are treated with more dignity than humans. The same spirit is working in both places but with different manifestations.

There was no sin in Adam, and his blood was pure and holy. He and God were one. Because of sin, our blood became corrupted and our DNA became altered. But God didn't leave us helpless.

He sent another Adam and gave us an opportunity to be born again through Him. Jesus's blood was sinless because he didn't receive His blood or DNA from any man. God designed the woman in such a way that her blood never gets mingled with the baby in her womb. It's always the blood of the father that the child receives. Who was the Father of Jesus? Jesus was not conceived by Joseph: He was conceived by the Holy Spirit. Mary only provided the womb and the body of Jesus. The Spirit, DNA, the seed, and the blood came from God.

That is why the prophet said that unto us a child is born and unto us a Son is given (Isaiah 9:6). The Child was born but the Son was given. Why is it the Child was born and the Son was given? The Child is Jesus and the Son is Christ. The Child was born through Mary, but the Son was given supernaturally.

To restore our original bloodline and DNA God instituted a process of being born again. We thought it was for us to go to heaven. Jesus said when we are born again we will only see the kingdom (John 3:3). When we receive the DNA of God we begin to see what God sees. He adjusts our vision or restores the eyes of our spirit to see His kingdom once again. If we haven't seen anything in our spirit, then according to Jesus we are not truly born again.

We are born again through Jesus Christ. We receive His bloodline and DNA. Hallelujah! That is why the Bible says that if anyone is in Christ he is a new creation and old things are passed away. Behold everything becomes new (2 Corinthians 5:17). A new creation needs to have new DNA and a new bloodline; otherwise it's not new. Once we are born again, we are supposed to focus on the new creation, not the things that are old and have passed away. Everything that is in Christ Jesus is in us now. Unfortunately, many still focus on the old things and talk about them instead of acknowledging what God has done for them, and they never make progress in their walk with God. They can't because they are still stuck in the old things.

We have three kinds of DNA: physical, emotional, and spiritual, and each part of our being is programmed or wired in a special way. We have a physical DNA, which controls the shape and size of our body. We have an emotional DNA, which is what we believe about ourselves, or how our mind has been programmed. And we have a spiritual DNA, which is the purpose of our spirit. We are very conscious about our physical DNA, where we came from, how we look, our nationality and family background, etc. We are also conscious of our emotional DNA in that we think a lot about our weaknesses and deficiencies. This needs to be reprogrammed. The Bible calls it renewing our mind, or repentance.

How do we discover the DNA of our spirit? When people came to John the Baptist and asked him who he was, he did not give them a business card with his name and address. He did not tell them whose son he was and where he was born. He replied to their question by quoting a verse from the Old Testament: "I *am* 'The voice of one crying in the wilderness: "Make straight the way of the Lord," ' as the prophet Isaiah said" (John 1:23). That verse was the DNA of his spirit, which was his purpose.

Jesus said, "In the volume of the book it is written of Me—to do Your will, O God" (Hebrews 10:7). There are many other prophecies about Him in the Old Testament. They were the DNA of His spirit. Everyone's life is written in the volume of the Book. There is a verse somewhere in the Bible that reveals the purpose of *your* spirit. Do you know the DNA of your spirit? It is the verse in the Bible that God gave you as your identity, or inheritance.

The more you acknowledge the new things you received from God when you were born again, the stronger you become in your faith and the sharing of your faith with others (Philemon 6). The Bible calls it the new man (Colossians 3:10). Whatever you focus on becomes stronger and better.

We must constantly think about and meditate on the new nature and bloodline we received. We need to disconnect ourselves by faith from the bloodline and nature we received from our earthly parents. That is a process of repentance and deliverance. We need to meditate on who Jesus is and what He possesses.

Deliverance from demons is only the beginning or the first stage of deliverance, not the end. When you are fully delivered you will inherit what you lost through Adam's sin. When you are fully delivered you will begin to manifest Christ on some level.

After you are delivered from sin, you need to be delivered from the religious spirit. To be free from the religious spirit, you need to uproot every Christian or religious experience you had until you discovered God's kingdom. The moment you discover His kingdom you start a new life. In the book *Kingdom Secrets to Restoring Nations Back to God,* I discuss the symptoms of the religious spirit. Please refer to those symptoms to find out if you identify with any in your life.

The religious spirit will cause you to believe that being poor is a sign of being humble, being stupid is wisdom, being clean is holiness, being insecure is polite, and doing the right thing will make you righteous. It will steal from you everything God has given you on this earth.

You then need to be delivered from your culture. How do you get delivered from your culture? By uprooting the mindsets that were formed in you by your culture and upbringing. Next, your country. How do you get delivered from your country? By getting rid of any pride about your race, nationality, and language. Then, your own self and your fears. Many people worship themselves. They think they are worshiping God, but they are worshiping Him only for their own benefit. As long as the God they worship fits into their plan and agenda, they will be happy. They tell God what to do and where to go. Instead of submitting to His will, they ask God to approve of their plans.

You need to be delivered from the spirit of poverty and the control of money. How do you get free from the spirit of poverty? You cannot cast out the spirit of poverty. You can only get rid of the spirit of poverty by giving what God will ask you to give, when He asks you to give, and to whom He asks you to give.

Most believers think that because they were not delivered from any demonic possession and they didn't roll on the floor and manifest any demons, they don't need to go through the deliverance process. That is deception. That's why we have people who are self-centered and self-worshiping humanistic beings, even in church! They are broke emotionally, spiritually, and financially. They divide and judge people based on their color, race, caste, language, etc. They are all waiting for the rapture or revival. Lord, have mercy!

When we are born again, we all become citizens of the same country. We speak the same language (which is faith), have the same Father, and adopt the culture of the kingdom. Unfortunately, when many people are born again they are taught that they are saved to go to heaven and they do not go through the process of deliverance and transformation.

Christians worldwide should have the same culture (the kingdom culture: righteousness, peace, love, and joy in the Holy Spirit) and the same language, which is faith, because we are all living in the same kingdom. We all have the same Father and are part of the same family. Most Christians are never taught about the kingdom of God so they remain rooted in their old culture and its way of thinking.

That is why Paul said that God delivered us from the power of darkness and brought us into the kingdom of His Son (Colossians 1:13). He did not deliver us and bring us to a church, but to a kingdom. When we move from one kingdom to another, we must learn a whole new way of life, culture, language, economic system, etc. Unfortunately, many remain in the same old kingdom and don't receive any benefit from the kingdom of God.

That is the purpose of the five-fold ministry. Such ministers are supposed to teach the body of Christ about what happened to them when they were born again. Instead of doing that, so-called five-fold ministers today try to build their own little kingdoms. They milk the saints until they bleed and prepare them to go to heaven.

Ephesians 4:11–15 explains to us the function of the five-fold ministry gifts. Their purpose is sevenfold:

"And He Himself gave some *to be* apostles, some prophets, some evangelists, and some pastors and teachers, for the equipping of the saints for the work of ministry, for the edifying of the body of Christ, till we all come to the unity of the faith and of the knowledge of the Son of God, to a perfect man, to the measure of the stature of the fullness of Christ; that we should no longer be children, tossed to and fro and carried about with every wind of doctrine, by the trickery of men, in the cunning craftiness of deceitful plotting, but, speaking the truth in love, may grow up in all things into Him who is the head—Christ."

1. Equip the saints for the work of ministry

2. Edifying of the body of Christ

3. Bring us all to the same unity of faith

4. Teach us the knowledge of the Son of God

5. Bring us all to a perfect man

6. Measure and stature of the fullness of Christ

7. Bring doctrinal stability and accuracy

If the minister of the church you attend has no heart for unity in the body of Christ, he or she is not a five-fold ministry gift. There are many self-appointed leaders and hirelings appointed by some *demonominations* (it's a new word I made up combining *demon* and *denomination* because all denominations are influenced by demons). There are more self-appointed ministers and pastors today than ever before. They call themselves to ministry and divide the body of Christ into another new piece.

All of the above points make up a step-by-step process. They are established precept upon precept to reach a particular goal. The goal is number six and seven: to reach the measure of the stature of the fullness of Christ and to have doctrinal stability. What is the fullness of Christ? It is when the body of Christ on earth collectively becomes everything Christ is. When we are able to manifest Christ is when we function as the body of Christ.

Now we need to study who Christ is. Unless we know who Christ is, how do we know when we arrive at the fullness of Christ? I hear from well-intentioned believers that they want to be conformed into the image of Christ. The question is, which image of Christ? How do we work toward a goal unless we know what the goal is? Christ is the Creator, King eternal, Judge of all the earth, Redeemer, Deliverer, Healer, Reconciler, Peacemaker, Wonderful, Counselor, everlasting Father, Prince of peace, Ruler of nations, King of all the earth, Source of all wisdom and knowledge, etc. I could keep going until eternity explaining who Christ is, but I want you to get a glimpse of what God wants to accomplish on this earth through His church. Each of us is created to manifest Christ in a unique way.

The body of Christ has been manifesting only a part of Christ instead of the fullness of Christ. That is why the majority of the world does not know Him yet. We love to heal the sick and cast out demons and prophecy over people. We broadcast it and shout about it, but that is not all there is to Christ.

When the body of Christ in a city collectively manifests the fullness of Christ, every demonic force will be under their feet. That city will be restored back to God. This is God's plan in all ages. The church has not caught up with God's plan yet.

When we know what God wants to accomplish on this earth and the purpose of the five-fold ministry gifts, we can all work together to achieve that goal.

Many leaders in the body of Christ do not understand the big picture, the eternal plan and purpose of God. They establish their own little kingdoms after their names and compete with one another to see who can take more people to heaven. They are trying to establish the largest churches and ministries in their cities and countries.

Comparatively few seem interested in bringing back the King, or what is happening in their own nation. As Paul said, all seek their own, not the things of Christ (Philippians 2:20). We will learn more about the five-fold ministry gifts later in this book.

The church is not about apostles, prophets, evangelists, pastors, and teachers. It is about Jesus the King and His kingdom. It's time for us to get out of the way and bring the King back to His original place in the church.

When we think of church, we should think of it as a nation within a nation. Peter said that we are a holy nation. A nation is something that has its own governing system, language, economy, culture, people, education, and agricultural system. Most don't think of the church as a nation. We think of it as a religious organization, living like a parasite that sucks life out of the world system and the country it is in.

In any nation, if the government comes against the church (I mean, if they push us to the corner), we will remain there and die because we don't have any roots in any of the systems by which this world operates. This is happening in many parts of the world.

Greater Things

Jesus said that we would do greater things than He did because He is going to His Father (John 14:12). What are the greater things? I believe some of the greater things are being the president of a nation, operating a business, traveling to other nations, etc. Those are some of the greater things we are able to do now because of what He did.

Because of the fall, man lost the following:

- Position

- Purpose

- Place to live

- Provision

Through the salvation experience, God offers all of these back to us. Don't limit your salvation to making it to heaven.

God Created Man to Rule

Whenever God created something, He spoke to that thing. When He created the animals, he spoke to the earth to bring forth all kinds of animals and creatures. When He created the fish, He spoke to the water. But when He created man, He did not speak to anything outside. He spoke to Himself. We came from God. Our spirit-man bears the same likeness and image as God Almighty. Because we came from God, we are supposed to be doing what God is doing. He creates something and then governs it. In fact, everything God created was made to rule over something else.

There were more people in the Bible that God used in the arena of government, and to influence governments, than any other purpose. Today, we have the least number of believers involved in or influencing government. There are more believers sitting in our pews that are called to be in government, and to influence government, but they have been wrongly taught or never taught at all about their calling and their purpose. They are frustrated and angry about what is going on in their nation and feel stuck. These people need to be released into their purpose and calling.

Every word God used in relation to our purpose is a political word. Jesus is a king. What is a king? He is a political leader. We are kings on this earth first. *King, ekklesia, ambassador, apostle, citizen,* and *reign* are all political terms. The Bible is not a religious book; it is the constitution of a kingdom.

The government was on Adam's shoulder. It means the management and rule of the entire planet was upon the shoulders of him and his descendants. God gave the responsibility to govern the earth to Adam and his children.

God sent another Adam, called the last Adam (1 Corinthians 15:45). The Bible says about Him that the government shall be upon His (and His children's) shoulders.

The government is supposed to be upon the shoulders of Jesus and His children (Isaiah 9:6). But the church has neglected it altogether and instead has been preparing people to escape the earth and live in heaven. In the New Testament, God gave the responsibility to rule and reign to Jesus because He is the last Adam. Jesus in turn gave it to His church.

In most parts of the world, people are waiting for another revival. I have watched some of the video clips of these revival meetings and I couldn't believe my eyes. Humans who are created in the very image and likeness of God crawled on the floor like animals and barked like dogs. I saw one woman leading a man, maybe her husband, on a leash, and he was crawling on his hands and knees like a dog. I put my hands to my mouth when I saw that. I said, "Lord, have mercy!"

When you manifest the kingdom of God, as it should be, people will run to get in. That is why the Bible says, "The law and prophets *were* until John. Since that time the kingdom of God has been preached, and everyone is pressing into it" (Luke 16:16).

Every person God used in the Old Testament is a shadow and type of Christ. Each of them manifested an aspect of Christ's redemptive nature. Moses was a deliverer; Christ is our Deliverer. David was a king; Jesus is the King of kings. Boaz was a redeemer; and Jesus is our Redeemer. We are supposed to manifest all aspects of the nature of Christ to the world in our day and age. We read in Colossians that all the treasures of wisdom and knowledge are hid in Christ (Colossians 2:3). The reason He lives in us is because He wants us to manifest to the world what is hidden in Him.

The Government Shall Be Upon His Shoulder

There were many in the Old Testament who witnessed God as King on the earth. They lived as kings, prime ministers, and statesmen. Why don't we see this in our day? Did God cease being a King?

> "For unto us a Child is born, unto us a Son is given; and the government will be upon His shoulder. And His name will be called Wonderful, Counselor, Mighty God, Everlasting Father, Prince of Peace. Of the increase of *His* government and peace *there will be* no end, upon the throne of David and over His kingdom, to order it and establish it with judgment and justice from that time forward, even forever. The zeal of the Lord of hosts will perform this" (Isaiah 9:6–7).

This is a prophetic declaration about our Lord Jesus Christ. It says that the government will be upon His shoulder. It does not say the economy, evangelism, religion, or business shall be on His shoulders, but government. Why government? If we lose the area of government in a nation, we will lose everything else: we will lose that nation. That is exactly what has happened all over the world. A nation rises or falls based on its government. It also says that of the increase of His government and peace there will be no end.

How does government rest upon His shoulder? He is the Head of the church and we are His body on the earth. The shoulder is part of the body, which means the government of this earth is supposed to be on the shoulder of the church. Throughout the Bible it was always a priest or a prophet who appointed kings (political leaders), not the other way around. For some reason we made this verse part of our eschatology, meaning something that is going to take place in the future. That is not true according to the Word.

That is what religion does. It steals from us what we should have now and gives us a false hope that someday things are going to be better. But faith says, "Now."

When we read the phrase, "From that time forward, even forever," we understand that the fulfillment of the prophetic timing began from the time the Son was given. It also says that of the increase of His government and peace there will be no end. That means it is eternal. We all know the Son spoken of here is Jesus. He came two thousand years ago and He ordered His government with judgment and justice from that time forward, even forever. It literally began two thousand years ago, but we have not grasped what that really means.

Witnessing Jesus as the King

The fulfillment of the prophecy in Isaiah began with the announcement of the angel to Mary, His mother.

> "He will be great, and will be called the Son of the Highest; and the Lord God will give Him the throne

of His father David. And He will reign over the house of Jacob forever, and of His kingdom there will be no end" (Luke 1:32–33).

When the wise men from the East came to see Jesus, they came looking for the King who was born in Bethlehem. How did they receive the revelation that Jesus was a King? It was because of His star they saw in the East. He was born a King and He died as a King, too. The inscription on the cross read *King of the Jews*. When the governor asked Jesus if He was the King of the Jews, He did not deny it. He said, "It is as you say."[3]

One of the complaints against the church in the book of Acts was that they were preaching another King other than Caesar and issuing different decrees.

> "But when they did not find them, they dragged Jason and some brethren to the rulers of the city, crying out, 'These who have turned the world upside down have come here too. Jason has harbored them, and these are all acting contrary to the decrees of Caesar, saying there is another king—Jesus.' And they troubled the crowd and the rulers of the city when they heard these things" (Acts 17:6–8).

How do we witness to others about Jesus as the King? Believers need to be involved in the political arenas of their nations. We have been avoiding politics for too long and the unrighteous have taken over governments all over the world. There is no such thing as a righteous justice system in the world anymore. People with money make their own rules. Any wicked person with money can do almost anything, anywhere in the world.

---

3 See Matthew 27:11.

Isaiah said the government shall be upon the shoulder of Jesus,[4] not on the shoulder of the devil. Church leaders should encourage believers to get involved in politics, both locally and in the central government of their nation. Otherwise, how do we witness to others Jesus as King? One of the main reasons this world is in chaos is because there are not very many people witnessing Jesus as the King.

---

4 See Isaiah 9:6.

Chapter 3

The Purpose of Government

"When the righteous are in authority, the people rejoice;
But when a wicked man rules, the people groan"
– Proverbs 29:2

What is the purpose of government? How did it all begin? The main purpose of government is to administer God's kingdom on earth, to work on behalf of God to execute His will and plan. Governments have been taken over by the powers of darkness to accomplish the will of Satan in almost every nation. The Bible calls them *rulers of darkness*. Most people in government are puppets in the enemy's hands.

There are thousands of believers sitting in our pews that were called to be involved in the government of their towns, cities, and nations. Because of the lack of teaching and training, they have wasted their lives and purpose. They are frustrated and angry with what is happening in their government but don't know what to do.

My intention for writing this book is to release those thousands of believers worldwide, and the future generations, to fulfill their purpose of being involved in the government of their nations.

When God created the earth, He gave Adam (and his descendants) the authority and mandate to rule. Where in the Bible does it say that God gave the governing authority to the devil or to the unrighteous? Where does He tell the righteous not to rule in this day and age? Where in the Bible does it say we have to wait until the millennium to reign on the earth? Reigning on earth is man's eternal purpose. From Adam to the last person who will be born on this earth, we all have the same corporate purpose.

Jesus was and is a King. The first thing the prophet said was the government shall be on His shoulder. He did not say the economy, religion, or business shall be on His shoulder, but government. A nation rises or falls based on its government.

The enemy knows this and for too long he has deceived the church to keep them away from government. Believers have been taught that kings are those who are in business. The noun *king* itself is a political term and not a business term. Who said kings can only do business but they cannot be involved in government? What an incredible deception!

That idea is based on an Old Testament concept and theology. In the New Testament, a child of God is a king, a priest, and a prophet at the same time. In our relationship with God we are His children, but our position on earth is kings first. What do kings do? They possess the land and rule, or govern.

I talked to a bishop from Nigeria, where a friend of mine was running for governor of a state. He said that Christians are afraid of politics so they won't come out to do anything. They sit at home and watch more TV. How is it that the very people who are created to make a difference for God are afraid to get involved in politics?

They say the political system is so corrupt and wicked that nothing can be done about it. If the political system is so corrupt, who is supposed to fix it if the people God put on earth and appointed are afraid and shy away from it?

When you study the Bible, you will see a pattern. God always works out His purpose and plan through governments and kings of nations. That is His method of operation. He loves government because He is a King and there is no authority apart from Him.

The main reason the enemy is doing what he is doing is because the church has given so much away to him and his children. We have rejected almost everything God gave to us, the earth, its resources, government, education, business, etc. Then we complain about what the enemy is doing through those venues. How is that going to fix or change anything?

For too long the body of Christ has been electing wicked people and appointing them in the offices of government and expecting them to execute righteousness. That is like expecting Satan to speak truth. He cannot speak truth because he is the father of all lies and when he speaks, he speaks from his own. Wicked people cannot execute righteousness because there is nothing righteous in them; that is why they are called wicked. The only thing a wicked person is trained to do is to be wicked in all his ways.

The Bible says that when the righteous are in authority the city rejoices but when the wicked rule the people groan (Proverbs 29:2). It is the desire and plan of God for the righteous to be in authority. Unfortunately, the so-called righteous removed or distanced them from any form of authority, and because of ignorance they have been hiding in a cave for too long. There is a time and season for all of us to hide in caves like Elijah and David, but that time and season is over. Now it is time for the body of Christ worldwide to come out of the cave and be who God wanted them to be all along.

God promised Abraham that nations and kings would come out of him. If he was called to be the father of many nations, there should be kings to rule those nations (Genesis 17:6).

The purpose of government is to establish God's will on earth as it is in heaven. For that to happen, it is very important for those who are in government to have a revelation of God, heaven and His will. Until that person knows how things are done in heaven, he or she won't be able to accomplish that on earth.

Releasing Kings to Their Original Intent

The reason most nations are going from bad to worse is because the people who are anointed by God to be kings are not occupying their place. The teaching that kings are those who do business in the marketplace reduced the capacity and the power of kings to

making money. This happened because of the influence of the spirit of mammon and the love of money. While they were busy trying to make money the enemy came in through the back door and stole our nation and families from us.

This teaching brought the love of money to the mainstream. Natural and common sense tell us that kings are those who rule and govern territories. They are not running around in the marketplace witnessing and praying for the sick, although at times they may do that. Their witness needs to be in the arena of government.

I am here to declare and release kings to the original intent for which God created them. When the kings take their place in every culture and nation, we will see the transformation we all have desired for so many years.

We have to train kings to be in positions of government and execute God's purpose in their regions. Churches need to remove the limitations they have put on the kings sitting in their pews and release them to be change agents in their nations.

There is a misconception among the body of Christ that believers are allowed to do business, play sports, watch and create movies, go to parties, and almost anything they want to do, except enter into politics. I wonder where that deception came from.

We have put people in office who don't even believe in God, or in heaven, and expect them to execute righteousness. It won't happen. For a person to govern, he or she needs a connection with heaven. Until they know how things are done in heaven, there is no way they can copy that on earth. Most people in government now are more connected to Satan and hell than God and heaven. The will of Satan and what they see happening in hell is what they are trying to implement on earth.

King of Kings and Lord of Lords

One of the names of Jesus is King of kings and Lord of lords (Revelation 19:16). Who are the kings and lords this verse is talking about? I used to believe it meant kings of nations, like England. Then the Holy Spirit opened my eyes to see that it was not only talking about those kings. God has made *us* kings and priests unto Him. Every believer in the New Testament is a king. Jesus is our King.

What does lord mean? The word *lord* means "owner"—someone who owns property. In England, there are lords in the political system as well; those who hold this title are called lords. Each believer needs to be a king and a lord; we need to own land, buildings, and intellectual properties.

When the Righteous Are in Authority

Every few years people go to the polling booths and put a new person in office, but the situation goes from bad to worse instead of getting any better. Christians will make comments like, "It's a sign of the end times or the last days." Believers have been saying this for more almost thousand years. Government officials lie, cheat, and steal the resources and development that are supposed to happen in their nations and in the lives of the people. Meanwhile, they increase the size of their bank balances and investments in foreign countries.

Is there a solution to these problems? The Bible says there is. The solution is for the righteous to be in authority. It is God's absolute will for righteous people to be in the governments of the nations in this day and age. It does not say for Christians to be in authority. All so-called Christians are not righteous, either. If a person is not righteous, there is no place for them in government.

Many leaders and end-time preachers taught us that these verses (Proverbs 29:2 and the verse in Isaiah 9) are talking about the millennial reign of Christ on earth. Maybe God forgot to tell Adam that he has to wait until the millennial reign of Christ to rule on the earth. No. People bought into that because they were influenced by the religious spirit and did not have a proper understanding of the Word of God.

God never intended for the wicked to rule this earth or to be in any position of authority. The government belongs to God and His children.

The solution to the problem we are facing on the earth has to begin with the church and then the governments of this world. For too long, because of the deception of the religious spirit, we have given the area of government over to the wicked. But that season is coming to an end.

Throughout the Bible we see that God raised people up to be in the place of rulership, or to influence the existing governments. He knows that the fastest and most effective way to accomplish His will on earth is through governments.

According to the Word of God the righteous are supposed to be in authority, but we have neglected this truth and it has wreaked havoc on the earth. Then we blame God and the devil for things they are not responsible for. All this time, we are the ones who have been carrying the keys of His kingdom.

And He said, "And I will give you the keys of the Kingdom of Heaven. Whatever you forbid on earth will be forbidden in heaven, and whatever you permit on earth will be permitted in heaven" (Matthew 16:19 NLT).

Another translation says, "When those who are right with God rule, the people are glad, but when a sinful man rules, the people have sorrow" (Proverbs 29:2 NLV).

Government Workers are Ministers of God

In many parts of the world believers think that if a person is involved in politics or working in government, they are not spiritual and not doing God's will for their life. This is a misunderstanding caused by the spirit of religion.

It is interesting to see that Paul calls people who are in government *ministers of God*. According to the Bible, whatever and whoever does the will of God are His servants (Psalm 119:91). He calls the angels who do His will *ministers*. That surprised me! I thought only preachers were called ministers of God. Why would God call those who are working in government His ministers? Because they are there to do His will. But not very many who are in government are doing His will these days.

God has anointed many people with His power to be witnesses in government but they have avoided it, thinking it is not God's will for them. Some, because of ignorance, leave their government and business positions and become preachers. Again, that is the influence of the spirit of religion.

The enemy has deceived us to keep us out of this most important aspect of our nation so he can have free rein. Every government on earth belongs to Jesus because there is no authority, natural or spiritual, except from Him. Why should we give the authority God gave us to the devil and then complain about what he is doing with it?

I am a minister of the gospel. I preach the gospel to groups of people. If you are in charge of finance in the government of your nation, then you are also a minister of God. You preach the gospel through your influence, your input, and your decisions. The same Holy Spirit is working through us, but in different arenas of life. It is interesting that in many countries people in government are called ministers; the minister of education, minister of agriculture, etc.

Each believer is anointed to manifest at least one aspect of Jesus. When we all come together as a body, we have the fullness of God.[5] Church, this has to happen. It must happen if Jesus is going to return. He is not coming for a church that is fractured into a million pieces and crying like a baby to get out of the earth. He is coming for a victorious church.

---

5 See Ephesians 4:13.

God's kingdom and dominion is for now and forever. Many are waiting for the millennium to reign with Jesus. You are destined to reign now on this earth. Jesus wants to reign on the earth through His church. We need schools in every nation that train people to reign, and to get involved with local and federal government. We have prophetic schools that train people to prophesy. We have healing schools that train people to heal sicknesses. Why don't we have schools that train people to get involved in the government and start businesses? We must act quickly if we are going to bring any change in our nations.

Why God Loves the Government so Much

It has been the plan of God from the beginning to dwell in us. Because of the fall, that plan was temporarily put on hold. David, because of his love for God, had the idea of building a temple made of hands for God to dwell on earth. He could not build the temple because of the blood he had shed, so the plan was given to his son Solomon. Keep in mind that the idea and the plan of building God a temple, or the tabernacle of Moses, was not given to a priest but to a king. Moses was not a priest. There is a specific reason for that. It is through kings and their governments that God wants to release His agenda on earth.

Throughout history, God always used a king to build the temples. They are the ones who financed the project. In our day, it is ministers or priests who have been trying to build the temple, and it is out of order. The church needs to release the kings to their original intent: to repossess the gates of governments. Only then will God's original plan be fulfilled on earth.

Solomon was the wisest and richest king that ever lived on the earth. He built a magnificent temple and set everything in order.

He appointed the priests to serve before the Lord. He appointed worshipers who sang about God's unfailing mercy. When everything was set in order, the glory of the Lord filled the temple and He came to dwell in it. There is a very important protocol we need to learn from this example.

We are all waiting for Jesus to come back to this earth. We want Him to come and dwell among us. But the temple for Him to come and dwell in is not yet prepared. He is not going to dwell in a temple made of bricks and mortar anymore. We are His temple: The entire body of Christ on this earth combined makes His dwelling place.

Now the body of Christ has been fragmented into millions of pieces, each piece claiming to be the perfect one. It is not habitable for the King. He is doing a new thing on the earth. He is beginning to destroy those walls that separate us. That is one of the goals He is trying to achieve through the kingdom movement. I deal with this more in the second part of this book.

We read in Ephesians 2:22 that we are being built together for a dwelling place of God in the Spirit. It does not say we are already built, but in the process of being built. When that building is complete, Christ will come to take His place and dwell in it. The glory of God will fill the earth. What is hindering the building from being completed? The kings have not been released yet to fulfill their assignment. When the temple is ready we do not need to ask or beg Jesus to come. He will come at the very moment the building is complete (Ephesians 2:19-22).

Just like Solomon the king built the temple in the Old Testament, it is kings that God wants to use to build His people in this day and time. Though we have scores of ministers across the globe, the body of Christ is not being built and edified. They are confused and lost because they lack the ministry of the kings.

That is the reason God is so passionate about government. He wants kings and priests (apostles and prophets) to function in their proper place and order. Though we are all kings and priests, each of us has a different function in His body. I wondered why God would give a dream to king Nebuchadnezzar, who was a heathen king, that revealed the entire future of the world from his time until the end. God also used king Cyrus and called him the *anointed one* (Isaiah 45:1).

Please know that Satan also loves the government. He knows that without the help of governments he cannot achieve his goals on the earth. He influences and puts his people in government to accomplish his will. Through kingdom government we will take the governments back from him, because government is God's idea.

Chapter 4

Responsibilities of a King and a Government

"A just king gives stability to his nation,
but one who demands bribes destroys it."
– Proverbs 22:4

Since governments are made of kings, I combined their responsibilities because they are connected to each other. Just as God taught everything else to Adam in the book of Genesis, He also showed him how to govern. He showed him the responsibilities of a person who governs the earth. We do not need to go anywhere else to learn how to govern: it is all written in the first two chapters of Genesis.

Manage

"The heaven, *even* the heavens, *are* the Lord's; But the earth He has given to the children of men" (Psalm 115:16).

God created man to manage the entire planet for Him. Man is in charge of the vast amount of wealth and resources God put in the earth. Man has to extract it and make use of it. Even after thousands of years, we haven't utilized or exhausted the potential this earth contains.

Cultivate

> "No shrub *or* plant of the field was yet in the earth, and no herb of the field had yet sprouted, for the **Lord** God had not caused it to rain on the earth, and there was no man to cultivate the ground" (Genesis 2:5 AMP).

God created the raw materials and gave man the capacity to imagine and make what he wants. That is why the Bible says there is nothing new under the sun. Man can only assimilate and assemble things in different shapes and order.

Teach

> "Come, you children, listen to me; I will teach you the fear of the Lord" (Psalm 34:11).

One of the responsibilities of people who are in government is to teach the people in that nation about righteousness, justice, and peace. These are the three core foundations of every nation.

Excavate

> "*It is* the glory of God to conceal a matter, but the glory of kings *is* to search out a matter" (Proverbs 25:2).

The majority of the wealth and treasures of this earth is hidden in the ground or under the ground. It is our responsibility to discover them.

Develop

One of the major jobs of government is to develop the nation. Anything we do in life has to continue making progress. We must strive for consistent innovation and growth. The moment we stop growing we start dying, whether it is a person, organization, business, or a church. The religious spirit will cause us to keep doing the same thing, the same way, for a century and rob us of the plan of God.

To Accomplish God's Will on Earth as It Is in Heaven

It is very important that the people in government have a relationship with heaven. One of the main purposes of heaven is to give us a revelation and make it real on earth. If the people in government don't have a relationship with heaven, they will not know about the will of God and how He operates. That is the number one problem with the governments of this world. They do not have a relationship with God, but instead are pawns in the hands of the enemy and do the will of their father, the devil.

To Serve Righteousness and Justice to the Poor and Needy

> "He will judge Your people with righteousness, and Your poor with justice" (Psalm 72:2).

Righteousness and justice are the foundation of God's throne (Psalm 89:14). Those two words are very important to God and

His kingdom. Righteousness, justice, and peace are the foundation of His throne. The wicked oppress the poor and take away justice from them. They cry to God for help.

Proper Management of Natural Resources

Every nation on earth has plenty of wealth and resources deposited in it by God. The reason many nations remain poor is the lack of management, or the mismanagement, of those resources.

Because of greed and selfishness, people steal and abuse the resources. Humans and natural resources are the greatest wealth any nation possesses.

Development and Management of People, Land, and Infrastructure

When you travel to some countries, it is hard to find good roads. What we think is a necessity in the West is a luxury in most parts of the world. The government needs to establish a proper education system to help people discover the purpose and gifts God put in them. Don't make people slaves to a system, robbing them of their destiny and their very life.

One of the differences I have noticed between a poor nation and a developed nation is the way they take care of their land. If we do not value the land, then we do not value anything else. Most people think money is the most valuable thing, but that's a lie from the devil. So, to make some money, they will do anything.

Work in Submission to the Church, the Ekklesia of God

The government needs to work in submission to the true church of God, not the religious system we have today that we call *church*.

Protect the Nation and Its Citizens

It's the responsibility of the government to protect the land and its citizens. Every nation has an army. Even the kingdom of heaven has an army. One the names of our God is Lord of Hosts. He has innumerable angels who fight and do His will at His bidding.

Responsibilities of a King

> "And have made us kings and priests to our God; and
> we shall reign on the earth" (Revelation 5:10).

Though we are called and created as kings by our God, we are not all created to be presidents and prime ministers of nations. That is quite impossible. The responsibility of a king is divided into ten areas of operation. Each believer is called and destined to be involved in one or more areas of these ten categories.

I will explain each of them below. As you read, please be open to the voice of the Holy Spirit to hear which area you are called to influence. As a king or a queen, you are created to exercise your gift and talent in one of these areas in your nation and to have dominion over that area.

1. Political Government

The first area in which a king needs to exercise his dominion is government. There is a common understanding or meaning that comes with the noun *king* in any language or culture on this earth: one who rules or is in authority. That is the number one responsibility of a king—to govern. He is in the office of government.

Adam was the first king on this earth because he was created to reign on this earth. Jesus, the last Adam, will be the last King and the King who reigns forever. If Adam (the first man) was a king, everyone born after him would naturally be a king as well.

There are believers who are called to be presidents and prime ministers of nations. We must teach and train our people about this. There are believers who are called to be governors or ministers of states, city mayors, council members, county clerks, and village officers. We should purposefully be training our people to be in places of influence.

In his epistle to the Romans, Paul calls people who are government, leaders, or rulers, *ministers of God*.

> "For rulers are not a terror to good works, but to evil. Do you want to be unafraid of the authority? Do what is good, and you will have praise from the same. For he is God's minister to you for good" (Romans 13:3–4a).

> "For because of this you also pay taxes, for they are God's ministers attending continually to this very thing. Render therefore to all their due: taxes to whom taxes *are due,* customs to whom customs, fear to whom fear, honor to whom honor" (Romans 13:6–7).

What a sad situation it is with the current generation, which has been trained only to have fun and pleasure. They are addicted to the things of Lucifer and bewitched by what he produces. They want everything for free and do not like to pay any price. They cannot see anything beyond what their natural eyes can see. Every morning they wake up thinking about what they are going to do to have fun. How much sugar and junk food can I eat today? Which movie is being released? Which sports team is winning or losing? That's the talk they spend the majority of their time on.

Kings don't think like that. When kings come together or have a council meeting with their elders, they are thinking about how they can expand their territory—which new horizon they are going to conquer, what they are going to do to develop the land God gave them, and how they can train the younger ones to reach new heights. That's how kings think.

Government is the major area of God's interest because He is a King and has a kingdom. He understands and is more passionate about it than we are. That is why He used more people in government, and to influence government, in the Bible.

There are different branches of government and political offices. If you are called to the government as a king, you are called to be involved in one of those offices at some level.

2. Land

Once you understand the kingdom of God and your responsibility in His kingdom, the first thing you realize is your connection with the land. If you have no revelation of the land and you do not feel any connection with the land you live in, then you do not have a full revelation of God or His kingdom. If you have no burden to care for the land you live in, truly you are affected by a religious and poverty spirit.

For a king, the land and people determine his kingdom. The size of the land shows the size of his kingdom. If there is no land, there is no kingdom. If an enemy has taken over the land, the king loses his kingdom. That is what happened to this earth. The enemy has taken over the land from us.

Even today, when false religious groups enter a new region the first thing they do is buy a prime piece of land to establish their center. They will not have a crusade or food distribution. They will establish a center and then they will start doing community works. I have heard that next to the US government, the Mormon Church owns the largest amount of land west of the Mississippi River in the USA.

The Bible says the earth and its fullness belong to the Lord (Psalm 24:1). At the same time, it says that if God's people humble themselves and pray and forsake their sins, then God will heal their land (2 Chronicles 7:14). Why does the land need to be healed?

The land was cursed because of the fall of man and the earth lost its power to produce to its full capacity. It stopped yielding its strength. Instead, it began to produce thorns and thistles. Sin and the shedding of innocent blood always corrupt the land. We need to appropriate the redemption we received in Christ to the land if it is to yield its strength again.

The devil will try his best to keep believers from owning any land. The biggest fight you will fight in your life will be to possess a piece of land. The first thing you need to do as a king and an heir of God on this earth is own a piece of land in your own name.

It is the responsibility of each believer to possess a piece of land and invite King Jesus to come and rule over that property and to release that property to Him, for Him to use it to reign in that region. This is not a 'me, mine, and I' philosophy. These are kingdom principles I am teaching you.

Once you own the land it is up to the King to tell you what to do on it or with it. Sometimes He will tell you to give it away to someone who doesn't have any land, or ask others to take care of it. He may tell you to establish a business, ministry, school, or nursing home, or to use it for agriculture. A farmer who is a believer and owns land and does agriculture is a king.

When Jesus shared parables about the kingdom of God, He shared about buying and owning land because there is treasure of the kingdom of heaven hidden in the land, which few understand. Everything you are and have is connected to land.

Everything we eat and use comes from the land. No land, no kingdom; no kingdom, no dominion.

> "Again, the kingdom of heaven is like treasure hidden in a field, which a man found and hid; and for joy over it he goes and sells all that he has and buys that field" (Matthew 13:44).

I was amazed by the above parable. The man did not sell everything he had to buy the treasure, but to buy the land because the treasure was hidden in the field. What was the treasure hidden in the field? It was the kingdom of heaven.

> "For the kingdom of heaven is like a landowner who went out early in the morning to hire laborers for his vineyard" (Matthew 20:1).

God wants you to be a landowner. God is the King of all the earth (Psalm 47:2). What is the earth? The physical planet. Why is God the King of all the earth? Because you need land to exercise dominion.

Every call and covenant of God is connected to land. It is our responsibility, as the children of God, to bring healing the land so that it will yield its strength once again to produce food to eliminate hunger from the face of the earth. There is land in most nations that is lying vacant and desolate. As kingdom representatives, we are supposed to move into these regions to make the wildernesses into a garden of life.

> "I will open rivers in desolate heights, and fountains in the midst of the valleys; I will make the wilderness a pool of water, and the dry land springs of water" (Isaiah 41:18).

"Behold, I will do a new thing, now it shall spring forth; shall you not know it? I will even make a road in the wilderness *and* rivers in the desert" (Isaiah 43:19).

"'I have raised him up in righteousness, and I will direct all his ways; He shall build My city and let My exiles go free, not for price nor reward,' says the Lord of hosts" (Isaiah 45:13).

"Those from among you shall build the old waste places; you shall raise up the foundations of many generations; and you shall be called the Repairer of the Breach, the Restorer of Streets to Dwell In" (Isaiah 58:12).

"For the Lord will comfort Zion, He will comfort all her waste places; He will make her wilderness like Eden, and her desert like the garden of the Lord; joy and gladness will be found in it, thanksgiving and the voice of melody" (Isaiah 51:3).

Less than ten percent of earth's land mass is inhabited. As kings, we need to move into those vast areas of land and build new, self-sustaining communities. People complain about the trouble and pollution in cities. Why can't we be like the patriarchs who established nations? As God's children, we are supposed to possess land and make it like the garden of Eden for the benefit of humanity.

"Because of the transgression of a land, many *are* its princes; but by a man of understanding *and* knowledge right will be prolonged" (Proverbs 28:2).

The above verse is powerful. One of the problems facing nations is division in governments, families, and churches. The above verse gives a clue as to the reason: Because of the transgression of a land, many are its princes. Though we are all kings, we are not all called to be leaders of nations. As kings, each of us is called to one of the ten areas mentioned in this book.

When there is so much transgression that has been done in the land, it is difficult for people to be united to achieve a goal. There will not be any unity. The same thing is happening in the United States these days. There is so much violence in our cities; young people are protesting and destroying public property. These young people do not know their purpose and are wandering the streets.

There is no unity in the government or between communities, and so much transgression has been done to the land and in the land that now the land is refusing to submit. That is another reason for the increase in natural calamities in this nation as well.

> "'Do not defile yourselves with any of these things .[please read the preceding verses in the Bible to find out the list of things that defile a nation and its land]; for by all these the nations are defiled, which I am casting out before you. For the land is defiled; therefore I visit the punishment of its iniquity upon it, and the land vomits out its inhabitants. You shall therefore keep My statutes and My judgments, and shall not commit *any* of these abominations, *either* any of your own nation or any stranger who dwells among you (for all these abominations the men of the land have done, who *were* before you, and thus the land is defiled), lest the land vomit you out also when you defile it, as it vomited out the nations that *were* before you" (Leviticus 18:24–28).

How can the land vomit out its inhabitants? Land is not a person or living creature, but the land has much more sensitivity than most people think or understand. The earth will itself testify of all the wickedness that has been done on it. Moses said that he called heaven and earth to be a witness against God's people.

"I call heaven and earth to witness against you this day, that you will soon utterly perish from the land which you cross over the Jordan to possess; you will not prolong *your* days in it, but will be utterly destroyed" (Deuteronomy 4:26).

The land can mourn because of the sins of its inhabitants (Isaiah 24:4–6; Jeremiah 4:28, 12:4; Hosea 4:3). When you buy a piece of land, make sure you redeem it from every curse that has been operating in it. Please *ask* its forgiveness for all the atrocities done on it. There are resources you can look up online that will help you do that.

3. Administer Justice, Judgment, and Righteousness

"A king who sits on the throne of judgment scatters all evil with his eyes" (Proverbs 20:8).

"The king establishes the land by justice, but he who receives bribes overthrows it" (Proverbs 29:4).

"The king who judges the poor with truth, his throne will be established forever" (Proverbs 29:14).

"Take away the wicked from before the king, and his throne will be established in righteousness" (Proverbs 25:5).

There are kings who are called to be judges in our nations. In the United States, people cause an uproar when presidents appoint Supreme Court judges, depending on their moral leniency. The judges uphold and defend the laws of the land. They define and defend the Constitution. What they decide becomes the final law of the land. They are kings of the land.

Jesus is a Judge. We need people witnessing for Jesus as Judge in our nations. Paul said in 2 Timothy 4:8,

> "Finally, there is laid up for me the crown of righteousness, which the Lord, the righteous Judge, will give to me on that Day, and not to me only but also to all who have loved His appearing."

We need righteous judges in every nation on earth. People are crying out for justice and righteousness. Corruption is a major problem worldwide. The church has been only talking and complaining about it for a long time. That will not make any difference or bring change to the situation.

What will bring the change to the situation is when believers who are educated in this field step up and play their role, bringing the change that we dream of. Believers make excuses saying that because the judicial and political system in their nation is too corrupt and dangerous they cannot do anything about it.

Imagine the corrupt nations Joseph, Daniel, Nehemiah, Mordecai, and Esther were living in. I do not believe our nations are more corrupt now than these nations were back then. Imagine living in a kingdom where the king was influenced by one of his assistants and issued a decree to murder an entire race. And then imagine God working to turn that situation around and the very people who desired harm for God's people are destroyed. We have not seen such things yet in our day and time.

> "Let the heavens declare His righteousness, for God Himself *is* Judge. Selah" (Psalm 50:6).

> "But God *is* the Judge: He puts down one, and exalts another" (Psalm 75:7).

"Rise up, O Judge of the earth; render punishment to the proud" (Psalm 94:2).

If our heavenly Father is a Judge, then we are supposed to be the judges of this earth.

What does a judge do? They administer justice to the people.

"He will not fail nor be discouraged, till He has established justice in the earth; and the coastlands shall wait for His law" (Isaiah 42:4).

4. Business and Services

There has been much teaching on the subject of believers being involved in the business world. It limits kings' involvement to that arena and calls it *marketplace ministry*. This has contributed to the current problem in this nation.

The reason Christianity and biblical moral values are in decline in the Western world is because people who are supposed to be involved in government are sitting in our pews, talking about things that have no eternal value.

There are kings who are called to be working in the business world. There is nothing wrong with believers starting and doing business. In some parts of the world, Christians believe that if you are a believer, it is a sin to be in business. This is another deception of the enemy. There were many believers, both men and women, in the New Testament who were businesspeople: Joseph of Arimathea, Dorcas, and Lydia are some of them. All of the fathers of our faith in the Bible were business owners, including the apostle Paul.

These kings are the ones who are supposed to create wealth to support the work of the Lord. They need to be anointed with the power to create wealth. If you are called to start a business, make sure you find an apostle and have him pray over you and commission you to go into the business world.

When people go into ministry, they are ordained or commissioned by other matured ministers. I believe we need to do that for all believers who are entering any field of influence. In the Bible, kings were anointed and appointed by prophets or priests. If that was needed then, it is needed right now as well.

As I mentioned earlier in this book, the enemy will not give up his hold on the wealth of this earth without a fight. You need the spiritual authority to break through those strongholds. I know many believers who started businesses but did not go anywhere, and some others that prospered and then had no time for the Lord. They are not able to win the fight on their own.

> "As sorrowful, yet always rejoicing; as poor, yet making many rich; as having nothing, and *yet* possessing all things" (2 Corinthians 6:10).

What is Paul talking about in the above verse? How was Paul poor but at the same time making many others rich? First of all, Paul remained poor in natural wealth because that was his personal choice. In the spirit he possessed all things and everything was at his disposal, but he did not let the things of this world have any hold on his heart.

Paul made many others rich because he had the keys to Kingdom Economy and lived by operating in the law of dominion. He commissioned and ordained believers in the Corinthian church to go out and make money. I believe he laid hands on and prayed over them for God to release the power upon them to create wealth.

It was to the Corinthian church that God revealed (through Paul) the secret of Kingdom Economy. He wrote, "For you know the grace of our Lord Jesus Christ, that though He was rich, yet for your sakes He became poor, that you through His poverty might become rich" (2 Corinthians 8:9).

> "And you shall remember the Lord your God, for *it is* He who gives you power to get wealth, that He may establish His covenant which He swore to your fathers, as *it is* this day" (Deuteronomy 8:18).

> "You are already full! You are already rich! You have reigned as kings without us—and indeed I could wish you did reign, that we also might reign with you!" (1 Corinthians 4:8).

I am sure it was Paul who taught them about their purpose because he established the church in Corinth. They received his teaching, applied it to real life, and saw great results.

The Corinthian church became a wealthy church in a short period of time. They reigned as kings. Wow! That's our purpose. They were not singing inside the four walls every Sunday morning. Nor were they waiting for a revival or rapture. They reigned in Corinth as kings. I hope you are hearing what the Spirit is saying to the church.

5. Establish and Enforce the Legal or Judicial System

There are kings who are called to fight the current political system of their nation to establish a righteous legal and judicial system. For example, in the United States there are many incidents where ordinary people went to court to fight for *justice* and the verdict became a law for everyone in the nation. Unfortunately, many times—or should I say, most times—it was the ungodly who were fighting to establish their evil agenda, and they won; and we have been paying the price for many generations. Some of the examples in the United States are Roe v. Wade, which made abortion legal, and Engel v. Vitale and Abington School District v. Schempp, which removed state-sponsored prayer in schools. Another group of kings involved in this arena are the police force and law enforcement departments of our nation.

6. Protect and Fight for His People

In a kingdom, the king goes out to fight against the kingdom's enemies. In our modern day, our presidents and prime ministers do not go out to fight wars; they just give orders. But there are kings who are called to be involved in their nation's army. There are hundreds and thousands of believers who are in the armed forces in our nations. They fight to protect the nation and people. They are kings.

If you want to know what kings and kingdoms do, just look at the devil and his children and what they do. He used to be a king and still has a kingdom. He enables his children to occupy key or high places in society and influence the culture and people. Where did he learn that? From our heavenly Father: the Great King.

7. Development

There are kings who are called to the development of a nation. Any development that takes place in any area of life or study is done through kings. Pioneers and entrepreneurs are kings. The reason many nations remain undeveloped is because the kings in their nations are not being released. They are singing in their churches about what David and Moses did. Kings, please go out and be kings in your country. God did not create you to sing—He created you to reign!

Heathens are not taught to sing in their religious systems, and they go out and make a difference in their countries. That is why the biggest businesses and corporations are owned by unbelievers.

8. Teach His People Wisdom

Another responsibility of a king is to teach the people in their nation the wisdom, knowledge, and understanding of God. These are kings who are the teachers, orators, and authors of our time. They bring out the hidden wisdom of God so people can apply it and solve their problems.

One of Joseph's responsibilities was to teach Pharaoh's elders wisdom. That means whenever Egypt had a problem that the elders couldn't solve, they went to Joseph to ask for wisdom and counsel.

> "He [Pharaoh] made him lord of his house, and ruler of all his possessions, to bind his princes at his pleasure, and teach his elders wisdom" (Psalm 105:21–22).

We read the same about Daniel. He was promoted to be the head of all the wise men in all of Babylon.

> "Then the king promoted Daniel and gave him many great gifts; and he made him ruler over the whole province of Babylon, and chief administrator over all the wise *men* of Babylon" (Daniel 2:48).

> "There is a man in your kingdom in whom *is* the Spirit of the Holy God. And in the days of your father, light and understanding and wisdom, like the wisdom of the gods, were found in him; and King Nebuchadnezzar your father—your father the king—made him chief of the magicians, astrologers, Chaldeans, *and* soothsayers" (Daniel 5:11).

The best teachers and the wisest people in any nation should be believers because they carry the Spirit of God in them. But I am not sure these days what spirit many believers carry. The moment they get *Spirit-filled*, they seem to lose touch with reality and this earth. In the Bible, when people were filled with the Spirit of God they always did extraordinary things.

I wonder if the spirit many receive is a religious spirit, or the spirit of this world, because most people love the things of this world more than they love God or His kingdom. They will create time for the things of the world, but they have no time for God. They wouldn't say that, but if you examine their lives and how they spend their time you will find it to be the case. There is little evidence of God in their lives in any area other than their church attendance. They live an ordinary life like any unbeliever.

Paul said very clearly that it is possible for a believer in Christ to receive a spirit other than the Holy Spirit. "For if he who comes preaches another Jesus whom we have not preached, or *if* you receive a different spirit which you have not received, or a different gospel which you have not accepted—you may well put up with it!" (2 Corinthians 11:4).

In the book of Daniel, we see that when the king's training was finished, Daniel and his friends were found to be ten times better in everything than the ungodly. That was also the case with the people of Israel. They were the head and were above the heathen nations. We have to remember that we received the same promise and are part of the same covenant God made with Israel.

The religious spirit has deceived us and stolen, or hidden from us, almost everything God has given to us. When we are free from the hold of religion we will begin to see the things God has prepared for those who love Him.

When the presidents and political leaders of our nations need help or solutions to the problems our nation is facing, they should want to look to the church. They should want to call ordinary believers who are filled with the Spirit and wisdom of God and ask for counsel. That is what God intends for and through His church.

9. Manage the Wealth and Resources of the Earth and Nations

"It is the glory of God to conceal a matter, but the glory of kings *is* to search out a matter" (Proverbs 25:2).

God has hidden every precious thing on this earth so that natural eyes will not easily find them. Precious metals and stones are some of them, but the greatest of all is wisdom. He hides these so only people who are very serious will ever find them. Kings need to search out and bring them to light so others can benefit from them.

There are many different types of resources on earth and in nations. It is impossible for me to list them all here. The most important resources are human resources. We need to help people discover their purpose and reestablish a relationship with their Creator. As a king, you are called to be part of managing resources for the establishment of God's kingdom on earth.

A king can recognize potential that is hidden in a person or on this earth. The above verse is very powerful. It is the glory of God to conceal a matter, but the glory of kings to search out a matter. God hides things so the kings can search them out and bring them to light. One of the ways kings manifest their glory is by revealing to the world the glory of God.

10. Recognize and Promote People Who Excel in Different Fields

It is in the very nature of a king to recognize excellence and promote it. They are always looking for people who excel in their work to appreciate and promote them. That is why the wisest man said, "Do you see a man *who* excels in his work? He will stand before kings; he will not stand before unknown *men*" (Proverbs 22:29).

There are many incidents in the Bible where a king promoted or honored someone because they saw the wisdom of God operating through that person. Kings will always appreciate excellence, wisdom, truth, and loyalty. Joseph, Mordecai, Esther, and Daniel are some examples of people who were honored and promoted by kings.

As a king, please make sure you take time and make room to recognize and appreciate excellence in people who serve you. Always look to bring out the best in everything and everyone. Kings influence and take over new territories. They require the best of the best in everything.

The Bible is a book of kings and kingdoms. It doesn't matter which type of government you live under: you can read God's Word and learn how a king and a kingdom operates. That's one of the reasons God gave us the Bible. The Bible talks more about kings and prophets than any other calling.

I am not an expert when it comes to government or politics. I write what is given to me by revelation of the Holy Spirit. What I write is to create an appetite in the hearts of believers and to open their eyes to the arena of government and their responsibilities to it—to answer the questions they have been asking and to remove the confusion and let them know that it is God's will for them to be involved in the government of their nation.

I encourage and charge believers worldwide to be a part of government and every position of authority in their nation, from the local to the top. Do not wait and waste your precious life, waiting for the rapture. I will say what Jesus said to the people in the parable of the talents: "Occupy until He comes."

Chapter 5

Church and the Government

"Let every soul be subject to the governing authorities. For there is no authority except from God, and the authorities that exist are appointed by God" – Romans 13:1

I know this has been a hot topic in our nation and time. Government cannot function properly without God. If it tries, it will become an instrument of evil in the hands of the devil.

Government needs the spiritual protection and covering of the church. In most parts of the world, the governments have been functioning without God. First, they need to recognize that all authority is from God. Without God, there is no authority. When the government pushes away the church, it is asking for trouble.

We haven't had very many able and mature men in the church that could balance these two critical areas, but from the beginning of time to today, we see an interesting factor: governments and God's people working in unity to accomplish God's will on earth. It is a *divine dance* or *divine partnership*.

Which is more important, the church or the government? I would say both are equally important because without the church there is no government and without the government there is no church. One deals with the natural and the other deals with spiritual issues. It's like Paul said: man is the head of the woman, but the man comes from the woman.

Throughout the Bible, we see God using both to balance each other. When one goes astray, God uses the other to correct it and bring it back to its place. In recent history, they began to work independently of each other. Government is doing its own thing and the church is doing its own thing, which has created huge problems in the nations. God never intended for the church and the government to work independently of each other.

People have argued for so long about the relationship between the church and government, the right procedure to follow for both to work together, and which one should submit to the other. There is no clear command in the Bible. They are supposed to work in unity, one taking care of the natural aspects of life and the other taking care of the spiritual. Which is more important, the spiritual or the natural? They are equally important and are supposed to go hand in hand and shoulder to shoulder, creating a formidable force and making it impossible for the kingdom of darkness to do anything on this earth. They are both supposed to check each other to keep balance and integrity.

Satan, knowing this plan, came up with all sorts of ways to divide the church and the state, as we call it in the United States. I call it the church and the government. The church is the one that is supposed to train good men and women and release them to go and serve in the government. The education system of a country is supposed to be led by the church, to teach people about Kingdom Education. If you do not know man's purpose, it is impossible to give the right education. That is what is happening at the moment in our universities and colleges. They inject our children's minds with all kinds of lies and brainwash them to believe everything that is against God.

Though they are equally important, the spirit has authority over the natural. The true church has authority over any government because the church represents the kingdom. But today's church doesn't represent God's kingdom; instead, it is functioning as a religious or a not for profit organization. When the church functions as God intended, it will exercise authority over everything else God created. Ultimately, both entities need to submit to God, acknowledging that from Him comes their authority and that both represent Him to humanity and are here to do His will.

In Daniel we read that the Most High rules in the kingdom of men. "...the Most High rules in the kingdom of men" (Daniel 4:17b; 25b; 32b; 5:21b).

> "The Lord has established His throne in heaven, and
> His kingdom rules over all" (Psalm 103:19).

There are times when the government should submit to the church, especially when it comes to decisions on moral and social issues. The government should heed the church. There are times when the church should submit to the government for economical and organizational protection and accountability. The church is supposed to offer direction, guidance, and balance to the government.

The church should be the one providing the government with the proper moral and spiritual foundation because the church is the one that received the word of God, which is the foundation of life for every society. Every government on this earth derived its moral and civil laws from the Bible.

The government should never dictate moral and spiritual laws to the church. That is what happened in the Middle Ages. Historically, when the church became corrupt, the government took over and used it for its own purposes and abused it. This is happening now in many nations.

Throughout the Bible, we see that it was always a priest or a prophet that appointed the king, the political leader. They received counsel and advice from the spiritual leadership of the nation.

We see in the New Testament that governments persecuted the church. At certain times, the church prayed and cancelled the laws and power of the government. God uses both the church and the government to accomplish His purpose.

We see in the Bible that during times of crisis or war, the king called the spiritual leaders of the land to inquire of the Lord as to what they should do. They received the counsel, and implemented it, and saw the solution or victory every time.

That's a perfect scenario for how the church and government should operate in unity and submission to each other. Apart from His voice and counsel, they did not do anything because both must be led by the Lord. They both belong to Him.

God is the one who appointed the government first. He is the One who delegated the responsibility to Adam to rule the earth. Just like marriage, God initiated it and without God it won't function properly.

The church is supposed to provide moral and spiritual support for the government. We need a new breed of politicians and leaders in every country.

Jewish people, though few in number, occupy key places in business, politics, and all other aspects of society. Why and how do they do that? They have a different revelation of God that we don't employ.

Surprisingly, the majority of Jewish people support the liberal agenda in the United States. They raise more money for liberal causes than anything else.6

Many uninformed Christians still think Jewish people are so spiritual and special to God; and act as though they themselves are second-class citizens. They don't understand that we have been grafted into the same promise and covenant.

We don't know how to tap into the covenantal blessings, so we wait for God to do what we are supposed to do. That is a very serious problem.

Why did God begin government on this earth? He wanted an organized group that was fully committed to execute His will and purpose on the earth. That is why He established government. Government is His idea, not man's idea.

---

6 See *The Jewish Phenomenon* by Steven Silbiger.

PART II

Church Government

Chapter 6

Church Government

"For this reason I left you in Crete, that you should set in order the things that are lacking, and appoint elders in every city as I commanded you" Titus 1:5.

W hy, in a book about government, is it important to discuss church government? If anything is to be fixed in our society, it has to start with the church. The church is the light of this world and the salt of the earth. When the church functions as it is supposed to, everything else will fall into the right place. Nothing breaks my heart more than seeing the church out of order, blinded, and groping in the darkness. As Jesus said, if the blind tries to lead the blind, they will both fall into a ditch and neither of them can help the other.

A nation goes in the same direction as the church in that nation. We are in the driver's seat, and God put an enormous responsibility upon our shoulders when He gave us the keys of His kingdom. He told us that whatever we permit on earth, heaven will permit, and whatever we do not permit, heaven won't permit.

In the following pages, according to the grace and the revelation that is given to me, I will explain how the church functioned in the first century. I hope you already read my book, *The Power and Authority of the Church*. This is a continuation of that book. If you have not yet read it, you may have a hard time understanding some things in this section. As you read, I ask that you eat the meat and throw away the bones. Don't get stuck on the nitty-gritty, but try to grasp the big picture I am trying to portray. I know you will be blessed.

Shepherd, Pastor, or Elder?

Though *pastor* is one of the five-fold ministry gifts mentioned in Ephesians 4:11 and is the most popular ministry title that is used today, no one in the entire New Testament was known by the title of pastor. We do not see anyone calling a church leader *pastor* as we see today. Whether a person is the leader of a church or other type of ministry, people tend to call them a pastor.

The Greek word used for pastor is *poimen,* which also means shepherd.7 Only in Ephesians 4:11 is it translated pastor. In all other places it is translated shepherd. Two of the three times it appears in the epistles, *poimen* refers to Christ (Hebrews 13:20-21; 1 Peter 2:25). I asked the Holy Spirit and He began to show me why. Jesus is the only Person that has the qualifications to hold the title of Pastor or Shepherd. Only one Shepherd is named in the Scriptures: Jesus. He is called Good Shepherd, Great Shepherd, and the Chief Shepherd (John 10:1-11; Hebrews 13:20-21; 1 Peter 2:25).

---

7 Strong, James. *Strong's Exhaustive Concordance*. Peabody, MA: Hendrickson Publishers, 2007. #G4166.

Every other place where the word *shepherd* is mentioned describes the *function* rather than a *position* or *title,* as in Acts 20:28. The people who were shepherding the believers had a different title. We live in a time when the most common ministry gift is considered to be that of pastor. If there was no pastor in the early church, then who *pastored* the churches and what were they called?

We need to look with a kingdom mindset at the church as the governing body of the kingdom. How does a kingdom operate and who runs the daily business in a kingdom? Who were a king's counselors, and who executed his will? What were they called?

In a kingdom, it was the *elders* who ran the daily business under the king. When the king had to deal with an issue or make a major decision, he called the elders of his kingdom to deliberate what to do and how to do it.

> "So Joseph went up to bury his father; and with him went up all the servants of Pharaoh, the *elders* of his house, and all the *elders* of the land of Egypt" (Genesis 50:7)

> "Go and gather the **elders** of Israel together, and say to them, 'The Lord God of your fathers, the God of Abraham, of Isaac, and of Jacob, appeared to me, saying, "I have surely visited you and *seen* what is done to you in Egypt" ' " (Exodus 3:16).

The Old Testament refers to them as "elders of Israel" (1 Samuel 14:3); "elders of the land" (1 Kings 20:7); "elders of Judah" (2 Kings 23:1); "elders of each city" (Ezra 10:14); and "elders of the congregation" (Judges 21:16). They served as governors and judges over the tribes (Deuteronomy 16:18; 19:12; 31:28).

It was the same in the New Testament church. Jesus is the King and He appointed elders through the apostles, and they functioned as pastors. They were called elders but did the duties a *pastor* does today. There was always more than one elder in a local church. Nowhere in Scripture do we find a local assembly ruled by majority opinion or by one pastor.

I have heard preachers refer to James the brother of Jesus as the pastor of the Jerusalem church, and Timothy as the pastor of the church in Ephesus, but I could not find any scriptural reference to support this. They certainly lived in those places, but there is no evidence of them being made the lead pastor over others there. However, there is plenty of evidence in the book of Acts that says the church in Jerusalem was led by apostles and elders.

> "Therefore, when Paul and Barnabas had no small dissension and dispute with them, they determined that Paul and Barnabas and certain others of them should go up to Jerusalem, to the *apostles and elders*, about this question" (Acts 15:2).

> "And as they went through the cities, they delivered to them the decrees to keep, which were determined by the *apostles and elders* at Jerusalem" (Acts 16:4).

When major decisions needed to be made, they were made by the apostles and the elders. The decisions that were made by the general council of the church in Jerusalem were addressed by the apostles and the elders, not by any senior pastor or senior apostle (Acts 15:23).

When Paul started a church, he ordained elders to run the church and they functioned under his leadership. It was always more than one person. "So when they had *appointed elders in every church*, and prayed with fasting, they commended them to the Lord in whom they had believed" (Acts 14:23).

Paul called meetings of the elders in different cities. "From Miletus he sent to Ephesus and *called for the elders of the church*" (Acts 20:17). He had an elders' conference like we have pastors' conferences today. He exhorted them to be faithful in the work of the Lord, saying, "Therefore take heed to yourselves and to all the flock, among which the Holy Spirit has made you overseers, *to* **shepherd** the church of God which He purchased with His own blood" (Acts 20:28).

It was the elders who shepherded the flock, meaning they did the function of a pastor but were not called a pastor. Peter called himself an elder. We do not find a hierarchy or a pyramid style of leadership in the New Testament. It was elders who were led by the Holy Spirit that shepherded the church.

> "The elders who are among you I exhort, I who am a fellow elder and a witness of the sufferings of Christ, and also a partaker of the glory that will be revealed: Shepherd the flock of God which is among you, serving as overseers, not by compulsion but willingly, not for dishonest gain but eagerly; nor as being lords over those entrusted to you, but being examples to the flock; and when the Chief Shepherd appears, you will receive the crown of glory that does not fade away" (1 Peter 5:1–4).

Gifts Do Not Always Mean Titles

Some of the ministers who call themselves pastors today are actually apostolic leaders of regions. Their calling is to raise up and appoint elders to lead the flock they have established. They should then move on to the next location to establish a new work. It takes godly maturity to release the people to do such work and leave the work they started. Most leaders like to settle down and keep people in their fold. I wondered how Paul raised up leaders in such a short period of time to run the churches he established.

There are others who are now pastors who were supposed to be elders, but because of insecurity and a search for significance they added a title to their name and called themselves to five-fold ministry. Some did it because of a lack of proper teaching. They have gifts, as every believer in Christ has gifts—but they aren't *the* gift of a five-fold minister.

If you are a lead pastor of a congregation and reading this book, I am not suggesting you should appoint elders and leave your position. It must be thought out and prayed over, and the congregation would need to be trained to adopt the change. I would say it will take anywhere from two to three years to bring that change. I write more about the function of a five-fold ministry gift in the next chapter.

Most ministries and churches today are built on a personality and not on Christ. If that person disappears or dies, that ministry suffers great loss. Our lives are supposed to be built on Christ, not on His ministers. Ministers, don't put yourself in the place of Christ. Lead and release God's people to Christ, who is their true Shepherd. You will have more fruit on earth and a better reward in heaven if you do so.

Responsibilities of the Elder

In the New Testament, every region had a bishop who had the oversight of multiple local churches. Timothy and Titus were such bishops who received spiritual gifts from the elders of the church. They were also apostolic leaders. That is why Paul left them or sent them to places to set things in order, as he would have done if he was there. "Do not neglect the gift that is in you, which was given to you by prophecy with the laying on of the hands of the eldership" (1 Timothy 4:14).

Paul told Titus to set things in order in the church and appoint elders. "For this reason I left you in Crete, that you should set in order the things that are lacking, and *appoint elders in every city* as I commanded you" (Titus 1:5).

There were multiple elders who were in charge of different responsibilities in a local church. There were elders who ruled and there were elders who taught the Word.

> "Let the *elders who rule* well be counted worthy of double honor, *especially those who labor in the word and doctrine*" (1 Timothy 5:17).

The elders prayed for the sick in the early church. When James wrote his letter to the believers, he told them to call the elders if anyone was sick. "Is anyone among you sick? Let him call for the *elders* of the church, and *let them pray over him*, anointing him with oil in the name of the Lord" (James 5:14).

Toward the end of their ministry, Peter and John called themselves elders.

> "The elders who are among you I exhort, *I who am a fellow elder*" (1 Peter 5:1).

> "The *Elder*, to the beloved Gaius, whom I love in truth: Beloved, I pray that you may prosper in all things and be in health, just as your soul prospers" (3 John 1–2).

Why would Peter and John—who were apostles—call themselves elders? There are no apostles, prophets, and evangelists in the kingdom, only the king and the elders who rule with him. In relation to the church, Peter and John were apostles. In relation to the kingdom, they were elders.

Each of the epistles was written to a particular church, not to a particular leader. Even the letters known as the *Pastoral Epistles* were not addressed to pastors, but to saints and individuals by name. Paul never wrote, "I write to the senior pastor or pastors of such and such church." We don't see that anywhere in the New Testament. If you study church history you will find that pastoral leadership, as we know it today, did not emerge until two to three hundred years after the church began. It emerged mainly because of the pagan influence of Rome. It happened when the church lost its kingdom mindset and apostolic doctrines and began to function more like a religious organization based on a particular personality.

All elders are supposed to be led by the Holy Spirit and all should have the mind of Christ. When that happens there will be unanimity in the decisions they make (1 Corinthians 1:10; Ephesians 4:3; Philippians 1:27; 2:2). If there is division, they should all come together to seek the mind of Christ until a consensus is achieved.

Why Elders?

As I said, the most common ministry gift functioning in the church today is that of pastor. There are more pastors today than any other ministry gift (and maybe all the other gifts combined), but it was the least-known ministry gift in the New Testament when churches were governed and shepherded by apostles and elders.

Why did God appoint elders to run the church? Keep in mind that God is a King and He wants to see His kingdom come to this earth, not another church. A kingdom is a territory ruled by a king, and he has elders under him. When a king in the Bible had a problem or needed counsel, he called his elders that ruled the kingdom with him. There were elders that were in charge of specific areas of government like ministers, secretaries, and commissioners of different facets of government. Moses appointed elders to shepherd the people of Israel.

> "So Moses went out and told the people the words of the Lord, and he gathered the seventy men of the *elders* of the people and placed them around the tabernacle" (Numbers 11:24).

Whenever there was a matter or issue to solve, they always went to the elders of their city.

> "But if anyone hates his neighbor, lies in wait for him, rises against him and strikes him mortally, so that he dies, and he flees to one of these cities, then *the elders of his city* shall send and bring him from there, and deliver him over to the hand of the avenger of blood, that he may die" (Deuteronomy 19:11–12).

> "Now Boaz went up to the gate and sat down there; and behold, the close relative of whom Boaz had spoken came by. So Boaz said, 'Come aside, friend, sit down here.' So he came aside and sat down. And he took ten men of the *elders of the city*, and said, 'Sit down here.' So they sat down. Then he said to the close relative, 'Naomi, who has come back from the country of Moab, sold the piece of land which *belonged* to our brother Elimelech' " (Ruth 4:1–3).

There are twenty-four elders in heaven, not twenty-four pastors or apostles. Why elders in heaven? They help God govern His kingdom. Only when the church gets hold of the kingdom mindset will it begin to have the impact God intended us to have here on earth.

"And He who sat there was like a jasper and a sardius stone in appearance; and *there was* a rainbow around the throne, in appearance like an emerald. Around the throne *were* twenty-four thrones, and on the thrones I saw **twenty-four elders** sitting, clothed in white robes; and they had crowns of gold on their heads. And from the throne proceeded lightnings, thunderings, and voices. Seven lamps of fire *were* burning before the throne, which are the seven Spirits of God" (Revelation 4:3–5).

"And the *twenty-four elders* who sat before God on their thrones fell on their faces and worshiped God" (Revelation 11:16).

Now comes the question: if pastor is a ministry gift that is mentioned in Ephesians 4:11, then why did the early church leaders hesitate to be called by the title of pastor? Keep in mind the church had been in operation in Jerusalem and in other places, led by apostles and elders way before Paul wrote the epistles to the Ephesian church mentioning the pastor. Paul was not establishing something new because he himself appointed elders in the churches he started as we read above. As I mentioned earlier, Ephesians 4:11 is the only place the word *poimen* is translated *pastor*; in every other place, it is translated *shepherd*. Following are the thoughts God gave me about this.

True Shepherding

To be a true shepherd is not an easy job. A true shepherd gives his life for the sheep. Jesus is the only One who did that, and to honor Him the apostles and early church fathers refused to be called pastor. Instead, they called Jesus their Pastor or Chief Shepherd.

"Now may the God of peace who brought up our Lord Jesus from the dead, *that great Shepherd* of the sheep, through the blood of the everlasting covenant" (Hebrews 13:20).

It is the duty of a true minister of the gospel to lead a believer to his or her true Shepherd. If we elevate a man or a woman to that position and call him our pastor, we can look at this individual as our shepherd instead of Christ. This is very dangerous. This is how many cults have grown. As long as believers depend on, or look to, a human being as their shepherd, they will not grow in their faith—and the body of Christ will not function in unity.

Any time you put your trust in a man or a leader *more than in the Lord*, God will remove that person from your life, or that person will make mistakes, which will break your trust in them. Jesus said not to call anyone a father (Matthew 23:9).

I believe the apostles and the early church leaders wanted to honor their Master, so they did not want to take His title for themselves. They did not feel worthy to be called a shepherd. They discovered their true and only Shepherd, and they wanted the people to know that as well.

"For you were like sheep going astray, but have *now returned* to the Shepherd and Overseer of your souls" (1 Peter 2:25).

Peter did not say, "You all need to return to me because I am your shepherd and overseer of your souls." He was pointing the people to Jesus Christ. That is what true ministers do.

"And when the *Chief Shepherd* appears, you will receive the crown of glory that does not fade away" (1 Peter 5:4).

In the Old Testament, God is known as the Shepherd of Israel (Psalm 80:1). David discovered this truth in his life. Though he had prophets and priests as spiritual leaders, he did not call any of them his pastor or his shepherd. He said,

> "The Lord *is* my shepherd; I shall not want. He makes me to lie down in green pastures; He leads me beside the still waters. He restores my soul; He leads me in the paths of righteousness for His name's sake" (Psalm 23:1–3).

The sooner each believer discovers this truth, the more blessed they will be in their lives. In turn, they will be a blessing to their church, community, and nation.

One Flock and One Shepherd

It is important to keep in mind that just because a believer is connected to his or her true Shepherd does not mean they do not need to be part of a local body. That is far from the truth. The closer you are to the Lord, the more you want to be part of His body. You cannot remain alone and be part of the body of Christ. No, an individual is just one member of the body of Christ.

If, after reading this book, you feel like you don't need to be part of a local church, you missed the real point and I have not accomplished my mission. There are churches that God has raised up that are doing what He wants them to do. God will use what He has to accomplish His will on earth. When the new kingdom-minded churches rise, the old ones will fade away.

> "Give ear, O **Shepherd** of Israel, You who lead Joseph like a flock; You who dwell *between* the cherubim, shine forth!" (Psalm 80:1).

> "And other sheep I have which are not of this fold; them
> also I must bring, and they will hear My voice; and there
> will be **one flock** *and* **one shepherd**" (John 10:16).

Jesus did not say that we would have many bodies and many shepherds, but one flock and one shepherd. Today, we have many different flocks and thousands upon thousands of shepherds. This has to change. If we do not change willingly, the time will come when we will be forced to change because of persecution. **Paul says the same thing.**

> "*There is* one body and one Spirit, just as you were called
> in one hope of your calling; one Lord, one faith, one
> baptism; one God and Father of all, who *is* above all,
> and through all, and in you all" (Ephesians 4:4–6).

It has been the desire and the plan of God from the beginning to be the Shepherd and King of His people and to dwell among them. For centuries it has been hindered, but at the end of the age He will see this accomplished. It is the ultimate goal (Revelation 21:3). I believe the kingdom movement will accomplish that goal.

The Old Testament echoes this truth as well. God spoke through the prophet Ezekiel against the shepherds of Israel because He was not happy with them. He told them He would be their Shepherd to lead and feed them and He would appoint one Shepherd over the flock (Ezekiel 34:11–21).

> "In whom [in Christ] the whole building, being fitted
> together, grows into a holy temple in the Lord, in whom
> you also are being built together for a dwelling place of
> God in the Spirit" (Ephesians 2:21–22).

> "Therefore say to the children of Israel: 'I *am* the Lord;
> **I will bring** you out from under the burdens of the

Egyptians, **I will rescue** you from their bondage, and **I will redeem** you with an outstretched arm and with great judgments. **I will take** you as My people, and **I will be your God.** Then you shall know **that I** *am* **the Lord your God** who brings you out from under the burdens of the Egyptians. And **I will bring** you into the land which I swore to give to Abraham, Isaac, and Jacob; and **I will give** it to you *as* a heritage: I *am* the Lord' " (Exodus 6:6–8).

Though Moses was leading them, it was the Lord who did everything for them. Moses couldn't deliver a fly. He kept talking about his weaknesses and never exalted himself as their deliverer or leader. He never said, "I am the one who delivered you out of Egypt and now you all have to listen to what I say because I am your shepherd." No. The Lord was their Shepherd. When Moses died, God did not even allow the people to bury his body. He knew they would make a *god* out of him or build some sort of altar at that spot.

Learning From the Israelites

As we read in Acts 7:38, the people of Israel were the church in the wilderness. Paul said that whatever happened to them was an example to us upon whom the ends of the ages have come (1 Corinthians 10:6, 11). There are certain principles we can learn from the Israelites and the way they operated.

First, though they numbered close to three million people, they had only one leader, Moses. He was the direct spokesman for God to the people. Whatever God spoke to Moses, he in turn spoke to the people. Under him were elders who met the needs and solved the problems of the people. Moses is a type or shadow of Jesus in the Old Testament.

The Roman Catholic Church is an example of this. Though they have more than one billion followers worldwide, Catholics have only one leader, the pope. I am not suggesting the leader should be a man, but Christ. But I sometimes wonder how they manage it and why thousands of priests worldwide choose to submit to one leader. They may not believe everything the way we do, but they have a revelation of how church leadership should function. They have their own problems, but I am trying to point out something positive. The problem is the Catholics put the pope in Jesus' place. They obey him more than they obey Jesus.

Can evangelicals have that kind of leadership in a right way, and what must happen for that to be realized? Just as the Catholics have the pope as the leader over their entire denomination, the Protestant church worldwide, including the five-fold ministry gifts, is supposed to follow one leader, that is, Jesus Christ, our only King. That is how we will all become one flock under one Shepherd.

What will be the testimony of the church to the world when that happens? It is because of the lack of apostolic doctrine and teaching, and the lack of understanding about what the church is all about, that different leaders rose up in the body of Christ. These leaders drew people after themselves instead of the Lord. Different groups sprang up, highlighting certain truths, teachings, and personalities, and many took them to an extreme. As a result, we created super-heroes, denominations, and mega churches.

In the early church, there were no superheroes. Anytime someone tried to be a superhero, there was a system of discipline to bring everything in line according to the divine plumb line. Today, we have no system of filtering or managing who teaches or does what. Almost anyone can do anything and still stand up and say, "Thus says the Lord." It was not like that in the early church. The rise of many leaders drawing people to themselves caused division and, eventually, the formation of different denominations under different doctrines and personalities. That never should have happened. Now is the time for us to come back to our one flock and only Shepherd, Jesus Christ.

Second, they were called a kingdom of priests and a holy nation. In Exodus 19:6, God says, "And you shall be to Me a kingdom of priests and a holy nation." Does that verse sound familiar? We are also called the same in the New Testament in 1 Peter 2:9.

Third, God called the people of Israel His army.

> "But Pharaoh will not heed you, so that I may lay My hand on Egypt and bring **My armies** *and* My people, the children of Israel, out of the land of Egypt by great judgments" (Exodus 7:4).

In the New Testament, the church is the army of Christ (Revelation 19:14, 19). Paul called his coworker a soldier of Jesus Christ.

> "You therefore must endure hardship as **a good soldier** of Jesus Christ. No one engaged in warfare entangles himself with the affairs of *this* life, that he may please him who enlisted him as **a soldier**" (2 Timothy 2:3–4).

> "Yet I considered it necessary to send to you Epaphroditus, my brother, fellow worker, and fellow *soldier,* but your messenger and the one who ministered to my need" (Philippians 2:25).

Looking to the True Leader

Many in the body of Christ are more connected to a particular human leader than to their Head, Jesus Christ. They are attracted to a person because of a gift or particular style of teaching or doctrine. In the West, children grow up watching superhero movies and their minds are formed with that concept. When they come to church as adults, they tend to look for superheroes instead of looking to Christ.

As humans we like to walk by what we can see, feel, and touch, but we are supposed to walk and live by faith. The body remains divided into segments depending on the leader they are following, so we remain ineffective. When the leader is gone, most of the people are gone as well. If they were connected to their true Shepherd they would not go astray.

Because we remain divided, we do not have a corporate voice or influence as the body of Christ on anything that is going on in our nation. Instead, every little group, with their little head, stands on the sidelines and watches the game the devil plays and talks about what he does. Enough is enough. Our greatest witness for Jesus, and the greatest tool of evangelism possible, is not the biggest crusade we can arrange on the National Mall or a football field, but the work we can do when the body of Christ becomes united as one. Then the whole world will know that the Father has sent Jesus His Son.

Jesus prayed: "Now I am no longer in the world, but these are in the world, and I come to You. Holy Father, keep through Your name those whom You have given Me, that they may **be one** as We *are* … That they all may **be one**, as You, Father, *are* in Me, and I in You; that they also may **be one** in Us, **that the world may believe that You sent Me**" (John 17:11, 21).

Jesus did not say the world will believe in Him because of the miracle crusades we conduct, or because we feed the poor and build mega churches in every city. No. It's time to open our eyes, wake from our slumber, shake off our ignorance and pride, get the religious spirit out of us, and read and obey what the Bible says. For that to happen, the current leaders need to get hold of this revelation about New Testament church government and how a kingdom functions and practice it in every local church. Then the transformation we are looking for will happen in the nations.

The mega churches and superheroes we see today will begin to diminish and eventually disappear. We are in that transition stage right now. There will be a falling away from these churches. There are millions of believers in this country who were once on fire for God and part of a church that are no longer part of a church. I read recently that there are 35 million believers in the United States who no longer attend any church. That is very sad. They became tired of what they saw in church, and with church leadership, and are disappointed.

Many others who currently attend churches are tired. They are not getting fed spiritually and continue attending a church out of Christian duty, but deep inside they have had enough. They still love the Lord, but they are weary and faint. It is similar to when Jesus saw the multitudes and had compassion on them, saying they are like sheep without a shepherd (Matthew 9:36).

Why does Jesus want His church to have plurality in her leadership? It is because He does not want us to get attached to a particular leader. He does not want any little *heads* competing with Him (Ephesians 5:23). He is the only Head of the body, and He wants the whole body to be connected to Him and depend on and trust Him for everything. He is the true vine and His Father is the vinedresser. Wow! Why would Jesus say He is the TRUE vine? Why would He have to add the word *true* there? It means there are false vines out there as well.

> "I am the true vine, and My Father is the vinedresser"
> (John 15:1).

"I am the vine, you *are* the branches. He who abides in Me, and I in him, bears much fruit; for without Me you can do nothing" (John 15:5).

Why is it most believers do not bear any fruit? They are spiritually barren because they are not connected to the true vine. They are more connected to their spiritual *guru* and a particular sect. It is a natural process for a branch to bear fruit when it is connected to the vine (John 15:4–6).

We are all part of the same body, connected to one Vine, one Head; including the five-fold ministry gifts. They are not excluded. They are different members of the body with different functions. In the Bible, we always see more than one elder in the local churches. I believe each elder was responsible for a different area of ministry.

"And He [Christ] is the *head* of the body, the church, who is the beginning, the firstborn from the dead, that in all things He may have the preeminence" (Colossians 1:18).

"And not holding fast to the Head, from whom all the body, nourished and knit together by joints and ligaments, grows with the increase *that is* from God" (Colossians 2:19).

The reason the body is dysfunctional today is because those who are called to five-fold ministry do not fully understand their responsibility. Many do not read or teach the following verses from Ephesians 4. Right now, the body is not connected to its Head. Ephesians 4:14 describes the condition of the current church very well.

"That we should no longer be children, tossed to and fro and carried about with every wind of doctrine, by the trickery of men, in the cunning craftiness of deceitful plotting."

The body of Christ has been carried about with every wind of doctrine by the trickery of men. Most believers do not know for sure exactly what they believe. When a new preacher on television says something new, one group will run after that man or woman for a while. Then when that person disappears, someone else will come with a different idea. As a whole, the body of Christ is tired, disappointed, and ripped off. Their hearts are broken; their lives are in shambles; they are financially ruined and emotionally wounded. They have been poorly discipled, and very few are being mentored. This has to change.

This will change when believers discover their true Shepherd and their only Lord. That is our Lord and Savior Jesus Christ. When Jesus saw the multitudes, He said they were like sheep without a shepherd. There were religious leaders at that time, and people went to the temple to offer sacrifices, but He said they had no shepherd. Those religious leaders were the biggest hindrance to people really connecting with God.

> "But when He saw the multitudes, He was moved with compassion for them, because they were weary and scattered, like sheep having no shepherd" (Matthew 9:36).

When the whole body is connected to the only Head, which is Jesus Christ, the following things will happen as it says in Ephesians 4:15–16.

> "But, speaking the truth in love, may grow up in all things into Him who is the head—Christ—from whom the whole body, joined and knit together by what every joint supplies, according to the effective working by which every part does its share, causes growth of the body for the edifying of itself in love."

Paul warned the believers about this in his farewell speech to the elders of the church in Ephesus. "For I know this, that after my departing shall grievous wolves enter in among you, not sparing the flock. Also of your own selves shall men arise, speaking perverse things, *to draw away disciples after them*" (Acts 20:29–30 KJV).

If we look at the body of Christ today, many leaders try to draw the people after them as Paul described. Some are doing it knowingly and others out of ignorance because that is the way they have been raised. The body of Christ will come into unity when these leaders humble themselves and train the people of God to have a direct and personal relationship with their true Shepherd and the rest of the body. The body has to be joined to the Head and they need to become one flesh for the real church to function as God has ordained.

> "For we are members of His body, of His flesh and of His bones. 'For this reason a man shall leave his father and mother and be joined to his wife, and the two shall become one flesh.' This is a great mystery, but I speak concerning Christ and the church" (Ephesians 5:30–32).

We have the same Spirit and the same mind that Jesus has (1 Corinthians 2:16; 6:17). A local body has to align themselves in such a way with Christ, removing anything from their lives that dilutes or contaminates that Spirit and mind. For this to happen, the teachings of Paul to the churches need to be taught and preached extensively. Believers need to read and meditate on the Epistles because they were written to the church.

Elders must be full of the Holy Spirit and wisdom to operate in their function. It's very hard to find such leaders today because of the lack of apostolic teaching and doctrine. We have too much flesh and pride of men operating in the churches. When a body of believers come together in the wisdom of God and are submitted to the governance of the Holy Spirit, Jesus will be very present in their midst as He promised. There will be nothing impossible to a local body of believers in that state.

Everyone's Needs Were Met

Believers in the early church sold their possessions and brought the money and laid it at the feet of the apostles. What did the apostles do with that money? Did they buy a house or a fatter donkey, or start a fishing business? No. They passed that on to those who had need, and no one suffered lack. Everyone's needs were met. What about today?

> "Nor was there anyone among them who lacked; for all who were possessors of lands or houses sold them, and brought the proceeds of the things that were sold, and laid *them* at the apostles' feet; and they distributed to each as anyone had need" (Acts 4:34–35).

They were not a stagnant body. They did not sell everything and wait around and do nothing. I am sure they received back a hundred-fold. After they gave to the church, they did not end up on the street begging. No. The Bible says, "Give, and it shall be given unto you" (Luke 6:38 KJV). They kept passing the blessing on to others.

A good example of this is when Jesus called Peter and Andrew. They toiled all night and caught nothing. At the command of Jesus, they cast the net and caught the biggest catch of their lives. But they passed that catch and their business on to someone else and they followed Jesus (Luke 5:4–11).

We read in Acts that they were witnessing everywhere and the church grew daily. The moment they developed a tendency to be stagnant, persecution arose and they were scattered. Wherever they went, they received from the Lord and passed it on to other people.

The Blessing of the Kingdom

The apostles also moved into new territories to witness for Jesus. They established the work and passed on to people what they received from the Lord, both natural and spiritual. They appointed elders and moved on to the next place.

> "And everyone who has left houses or brothers or sisters or father or mother or wife or children or lands, for My name's sake, shall receive a hundredfold, and inherit eternal life" (Matthew 19:29).

These days, some people use this verse to ask for a hundred houses and other material things as if that is what Jesus was talking about. He was not just talking about material possessions, but brothers, sisters, father, wife, children, and others. How do we receive a hundred fathers, mothers, brothers, and sisters? Through the people we influence in our ministry journey.

Throughout my ministry journey, people have received me into their homes as their family member and I have stayed with them multiple times. I enjoyed being with them as if I were in my own house for as long as I was there. Wherever I went, God gave me brothers, sisters, and people whom I love as my father or mother. They treat me as their son. What a blessing it is! Even now, since my natural father and mother died, God has brought others into my life that I call Papa and Mom. I know hundreds of brothers and sisters around the world.

We do not see any of the apostles having a hundred houses and fishing boats and donkeys. Why? Did they not understand and receive what Jesus promised them? Yes, they did, but not with the charismatic or materialistic spirit we have today.

> "As unknown, and *yet* well known; as dying, and behold we live; as chastened, and *yet* not killed; as sorrowful, yet always rejoicing; **as poor, yet making many rich; as having nothing, and** *yet* **possessing all things**" (2 Corinthians 6:9–10).

It is important we understand these verses. Paul is saying that although he lived as poor, he made many people rich. How does a person make others rich if he himself is poor? That sounds impossible, but not to a true apostolic minister because his responsibility is to receive from the Lord and pass it on to others. Apostles are pioneers; in the spirit they go before and make a way where there is no way.

Apostles open up realms and resources in the spirit and for the believers to walk in and receive, and then they move on because in the spirit an apostle possesses all things. They are a type of a father. They labor in the spirit so their spiritual children can enjoy the blessings their heavenly Father has stored for them. They reveal to the church what God has made available to them through Christ, the glorious riches of His inheritance, both natural and spiritual, and then the church steps in and receives them and passes them on to those who are in need. This cycle must continue for the body to grow and be healthy and be a blessing to their communities. I am speaking of all these things spiritually. These are gifts that are spiritually discerned and not carnal in nature. Carnally, this process will not make sense.

> "Therefore let no one boast in men. **For all things are yours:** whether Paul or Apollos or Cephas, or the world or life or death, or things present or things to come—all

are yours. And you *are* Christ's, and Christ *is* God's" (1 Corinthians 3:21–23).

We are co-heirs with Jesus (Romans 8:16–17). He has made all things available to us for free. That is why this verse says, "All things are yours, the world, life or death, things present or things to come—all are yours" (see also Romans 8:32; 1 Corinthians 2:12).

This works in reverse order today. So-called apostles twist the hands of the people and steal what the believers have to buy a bigger house or a nicer car. Most believers remain poor and broke while the minister is getting richer and richer and the people out there are dying and going to hell. Then the next week, the minister will come up with another idea to get more money from the believers and fleece them a little more. Meanwhile, the church as a whole remains ineffective and believers remain broke emotionally and financially. This happens because the so-called minister does not know how a five-fold ministry gift should operate.

There are many false apostles and prophets today, as in the first century. They draw the attention of the flock to themselves by deceiving people. In fact, they themselves are sometimes deceived, believing they are serving God. They are wolves in sheep's clothing, tearing the sheep into pieces. Anyone anywhere who claims to be an apostle or a minister of Jesus Christ and draws the people to himself rather than to Jesus, and uses people to increase his or her personal wealth, is not a true minister of God.

> "I know your works, your labor, your patience, and that you cannot bear those who are evil. And you have tested those who say they *are apostles and are not*, and have found them liars" (Revelation 2:2).

> "For such *are* false apostles, deceitful workers, transforming themselves into apostles of Christ. And no

wonder! For Satan himself transforms himself into an angel of light" (2 Corinthians 11:13–14).

Jesus and Paul are our examples of a five-fold ministry gift. The way Jesus functioned and did ministry should be our model. Whatever He received from the Father He, in turn, gave to the disciples and the rest of us (John 17:7). That is the example the early apostles followed. We should not change it for our personal gain or glory.

Chapter 7

Five-Fold Ministry Gifts

"And He Himself gave some to be apostles, some prophets,
some evangelists, and some pastors and teachers"
– Ephesians 4:11

In many parts of the world, and in many churches, when a believer discovers his or her spiritual gift they think they are called to full-time ministry. Many leave the local church they are attending and move to the other side of the street and open another religious center, which they call a church. This happens because of the lack of proper teaching and apostolic doctrine in the church.

Another reason people enter into ministry is to compensate for their insecurity and feeling of insignificance. Everyone wants to feel significant and important. What better thing could they do to get the recognition and approval of people than start a church? In some parts of the world people enter into ministry to make a livelihood. Paul tells us they serve their belly and that is their god (Romans 16:18; Philippians 3:19).

Every member of the body has received at least one spiritual gift. That doesn't mean they are all called to the five-fold ministry. Jesus said these signs shall follow those who believe. The only requirement for doing signs and wonders or healing the sick or casting out demons is to believe (Mark 16:17). That won't make you an apostle.

Five-Fold Ministry Gifts

The five-fold ministry gifts are mentioned in Ephesians 4:11. Jesus has appointed some apostles, prophets, evangelists, pastors, and teachers to establish churches, to equip the saints for the work of the ministry, and to maintain the unity in the body of Christ.

Only some people are called into these offices. A believer cannot assume he is called into this ministry. Jesus directly calls and appoints these ministers. You do not pick what you like in this case and appoint yourself to be a minister of the gospel. Everyone is called to share the gospel. If you are a believer, you have a responsibility to share the gospel, help the poor, and pray for the sick. That does not mean you are called to one of the five-fold ministry gifts.

This can be confusing. Just because we are good at sharing the gospel does not make us evangelists. If you have a healing gift, that does not make you an apostle. If you have intuition and discernment about other people's lives, situations, and circumstances, that does not make you a prophet.

If you are a child of God, you are supposed to hear from Him. Signs and wonders are supposed to follow all who believe (Mark 16:17–18). You do not need to be called into five-fold ministry to hear from God. If you are good with people and know how to be around them, that does not mean you are called to be a pastor. You may have the ability to teach, but you may not be called to be a teacher in the church.

How do you know if you are called to one of the five-fold ministry gifts? It is very simple—just answer the following questions: When did God call you? What exactly did He say when He called you? What did He ask you to do? If we look at the life of Paul and how he was called, we will learn some valuable lessons. In Acts 26:14–18 we see that God communicated clearly and directly to Paul concerning his call, and He continued to communicate clearly with him about what he was supposed to be doing after that, too.

When Jesus called His disciples, He told them what they would become and what they would do. Let me tell you frankly: God does not call you through another man to be in five-fold ministry. He might use others to confirm what He has already told you or what is in your heart. God speaks to you directly if He wants you to be in the five-fold ministry. You must hear from God for yourself.

For instance, someone could hear the word *go* and assume they are supposed to be missionaries to China. Many people create *a paragraph* out of *a word* they hear from God. They add their own ideas and interpretations to it to shape it into what they *would like to hear* God speak to them. Then they try to make things happen. After a few years, they realize that what they are trying to do is not working. Then they wonder if they really heard from God or not. Even if they realize they have added to God's command, some will not stop what they are doing because of their pride. They don't want to admit that they were wrong.

The purpose and function of these ministry gifts is outlined in the following verses.

> "For the equipping of the saints for the work of ministry, for the edifying of the body of Christ, till we all come to the unity of the faith and of the knowledge of the Son of God, to a perfect man, to the measure of the stature

of the fullness of Christ; that we should no longer be children, tossed to and fro and carried about with every wind of doctrine, by the trickery of men, in the cunning craftiness of deceitful plotting, but, speaking the truth in love, may grow up in all things into Him who is the head—Christ—from whom the whole body, joined and knit together by what every joint supplies, according to the effective working by which every part does its share, causes growth of the body for the edifying of itself in love" (Ephesians 4:12–16).

I explained in a previous chapter the purpose of the five-fold ministry gifts. Please make sure you read and study it.

The Function of a Five-Fold Ministry Gift

If you are called to five-fold ministry you have a very specific and peculiar calling. First, you are not supposed to draw the attention of people to yourself. Anytime you become more important to people than Jesus, you are in error. If the body of Christ is to come into unity, then the leaders have to lead others to Jesus and get out of the way. Anytime people paid more attention to the apostles or were getting ready to give them the praise and the glory that belonged to Jesus, they stopped the people from doing it.

Second, once you establish a work you are supposed to appoint elders to run that local body. Third, you are not supposed to settle down in a place; once you appoint leaders, you need to move on to another place. At least this is the way it should be done and was done in the early church. This process of church planting should continue until your ministry on this earth is over. This principle applies to all five-fold ministry gifts, not just apostles.

The primary purpose of the five-fold ministry gifts is to equip the saints. When leaders settled down and began to establish their own little kingdoms rather than the kingdom of Jesus Christ, problems developed. Leaders had a certain number of followers and reigned as their *god*. If you look at the lives of these ministers, many of them did not end well. At some point in their lives, they began to focus on themselves for survival or prominence rather than Jesus Christ. Because they settled down in one place, their work was also limited. Unfortunately, this has become the norm today.

Look at the army of any nation. If you are a soldier, your leaders will not let you be stationed in one place for a long period of time. Whether you have a family, children, or whether your grandma is living with you or not, they will move you to places and countries where there is a need. When the order is issued, you either move or you resign and go home. There is no room for negotiation.

The body of Christ is supposed to work like this: Five-fold ministry gifts are pioneers. They go ahead and clear the path for the rest of the body to follow. We receive from the Lord and pass it on to the people, and in turn the people are supposed to pass it on to the ones who come after them. That is discipleship. It works like a chain reaction. This includes both material and spiritual things.

> "For I received from the Lord that which I also delivered to you" (1 Corinthians 11:23a).

> "For I delivered to you first of all that which I also received" (1 Corinthians 15:3a).

When we settle down, the flow stops. Then we have to use all kinds of gimmicks to raise money to survive. We are not supposed to be stagnant. As long as we continue moving, God continues to flow through us. The Roman Catholic Church has one leader, the pope. It does not matter how wonderful and charismatic a local priest might be, he will not try to establish a ministry for himself in his name. He always works in submission to the church and the pope. Roman Catholics have respect for their church and their leader. I believe that is something we should aspire to learn from them.

The whole body is supposed to be under one leader, one Head, and one Shepherd. Our pope is supposed to be Jesus and not any man. Jesus is supposed to be the center of our focus. He has the preeminence in everything, and no man can take His glory. Jesus is the Cornerstone of the church. Jesus is the Head of the church. Our Shepherd, our Bridegroom, our Healer, you name it: everything is Jesus and for Jesus and about Jesus. When you remove Jesus from being our one and only Lord, things get out of order.

> "And He is the head of the body, the church, who is the beginning, the firstborn from the dead, that *in all things* He may have *the preeminence*" (Colossians 1:18).

We need change. True apostolic ministry has to arise. What was Paul's response to the believers when they developed a tendency to gravitate toward a particular leader rather than Christ, and begin groups? Let's read and find out.

> "For it has been declared to me concerning you, my brethren, by those of Chloe's *household,* that there are contentions among you. Now I say this, that each of you says, 'I am of Paul,' or 'I am of Apollos,' or 'I am of Cephas,' or 'I am of Christ.' Is Christ divided? Was Paul crucified for you? Or were you baptized in the name of Paul?" (1 Corinthians 1:11–13).

> "And I, brethren, could not speak to you as to spiritual *people* but as to carnal, as to babes in Christ. I fed you with milk and not with solid food; for until now you

were not able *to receive it,* and even now you are still not able; for you are still carnal. For where *there are* envy, strife, and divisions among you, are you not carnal and behaving like *mere* men? For when one says, 'I am of Paul,' and another, 'I *am* of Apollos,' are you not carnal?" (1 Corinthians 3:1–4).

Wow! Paul says that when believers gravitate toward a particular leader to form a group, or division, they become carnal. What do you think of the present condition of the church? Is it carnal or spiritual?

"Who then is Paul, and who *is* Apollos, but ministers through whom you believed, as the Lord gave to each one? I planted, Apollos watered, but God gave the increase. So then neither he who plants is anything, nor he who waters, but God who gives the increase. Now he who plants and he who waters are one, and each one will receive his own reward according to his own labor. For we are God's fellow workers; you are God's field, *you are* God's building" (1 Corinthians 3:5–9).

This might sound far off when you read it because the church has come a long way from her original mission and function. We are used to watching superhero movies and following celebrities. In the early days, people tried to deify the apostles and worship them as gods (Acts 14:11–12).

One of the functions of five-fold ministry gifts is to bring unity to the body of Christ. This is not happening today, as it should. Instead of bringing unity, many cause division because they settle down in one place and try to build an empire for themselves. Out of this came all of the denominations and sects we now have. Each denomination specialized in a particular doctrine or teaching from the Bible, or followed a particular leader. We are supposed to be one body—not many fragments. As a result, each fragment of the body of Christ has leaders who have great influence in their little part, but the whole body lacks in unity and vision because the leaders are not united in a real way.

Now we have four different churches on the four corners of the same street. All of them are trying to do the same thing. They are trying to establish the largest church in town, win the lost, feed the hungry, start schools, etc. They don't want to work together but what if they joined forces? What if they combined their resources and worked together? They would achieve their goals faster and become more effective in what they are trying to do.

They are not working together because of either a lack of understanding and maturity or because they are influenced by the same spirit of this world that influenced men to build the Tower of Babel. God came down and sent confusion, dispersing them to the four corners of the earth.

> "I, therefore, the prisoner of the Lord, beseech you to walk worthy of the calling with which you were called, with all lowliness and gentleness, with longsuffering, bearing with one another in love, endeavoring to keep the unity of the Spirit in the bond of peace. *There is* **one body and one Spirit, just as you were called in one hope of your calling; one Lord, one faith, one baptism; one God** and Father of all, who *is* above all, and through all, and in you all" (Ephesians 4:1–6).

The Two Types of Five-Fold Ministry Gifts

There are two types of five-fold ministry gifts. The first consists of those who are called primarily to minister to the body of Christ. The second group consists of those who are called to primarily reach unbelievers. How do you know the difference? If you are called primarily to minister to the body of Christ, your messages and revelations will be from the epistles Paul wrote to the churches.

Your passion will be to see believers walk in victory and become everything God intended them to be. You are passionate to see the church walk in the power and authority God has given her. Nothing else will satisfy you. The messages and revelations God gives you will be for the entire body of Christ, not just a local congregation. This person's ministry transcends cultures and languages. He or she is a gift to the world at large.

If you are called to minister primarily to unbelievers, your messages and revelations will be primarily from the Gospels. Your passion is to see the gospel preached and people coming to Christ. You want to share the gospel with everyone you meet. The gospel is for the entire human race, so this person's ministry is also for the entire world.

If you are a believer who is not called to five-fold ministry, but have a gift of exhortation, your messages will be for one local body for that particular time. Many of your words will spring from the stories of different characters in the Bible.

How does a person know whether he or she is called into five-fold ministry? Below I mention twenty-one qualities that are traits of the five-fold ministry gifts. This list will help you know whether a person is called into them.

There are different types of callings and gifts. We read in Romans 11:29 that the gifts and calling of God are without repentance (KJV). All apostles are not the same and do not have the same kind of ministry. It is the same with the others.

"There are diversities of gifts, but the same Spirit. There are differences of ministries, but the same Lord. And there are diversities of activities, but it is the same God who works all in all" (1 Corinthians 12:4–6).

In natural government, there are different levels of authority. Everyone who works in the government does not carry the same authority. In the Indian government, we call our leaders *ministers.* We have state-level ministers and central government ministers with the same title, but the central level has greater responsibility than the state level, even though it carries a similar title. That means every state has a minister of transportation that is responsible only for that particular state.

The minister that is responsible for one state does not have any jurisdiction in any other state. Just because someone is a minister of transportation in the state of Kerala does not mean he can go to the state of Punjab and exercise that same authority. If he tries to do that, the people will throw him out of their state.

But we also have a minister of transportation in the central government that is responsible for overseeing transportation over the whole country. He can go to any state and exercise his authority. Other ministers are elected to deal with defense, health, education, and international relationships. Spiritual ministry works the same way. There are apostles who are called to a locality, others are called to a whole state, and still others are called to an entire nation. There are also a few who are called to minister at an international level.

There are elders/pastors who are called to lead a church of fifty people, twenty-five people and up to 25,000 people or more. Again, it's not the number that matters but how effective the body is in administering the kingdom of God. It is all part of the calling and according to the way the Holy Spirit has distributed His gifts and authority. We are all ministers of the same God but with different operations. It is the same with all levels of ministry. We need to find out the place of our assignment. That is our spiritual jurisdiction.

The following qualities will determine whether a person is called into five-fold ministry.

Direct Communication from God

From the beginning of time, when God needed someone to do something He communicated with that person. We call it *the call of God*. This is especially true of five-fold ministry. No one calls himself into ministry. A call to ministry is determined by God before a person is born. One of the most repeated testimonies of people we read about in the Bible is that they were called from their mother's womb.

The Bible says God called or knew Isaiah, Jeremiah, Paul, and John the Baptist before they were born (Isaiah 49:1; Jeremiah 1:5; Galatians 1:15; Luke 1:13). The Bible is a history of these people who were foreknown by God. If we study their lives, a common thread is that God directly told them or their parents about their purpose or assignment. This also includes Samson and Josiah and others. During the course of life, there will be some incident through which God will communicate to those called to five-fold ministry. It can happen at any age.

Spiritual Authority

God will equip those who are called into five-fold ministry with a level of authority that is not seen in all believers. Ministers face more spiritual battles than other believers and they need extra authority to deal with those spiritual forces. When you listen to them speak or minister, you can sense the authority God has vested in them.

One of the distinguishing elements that the Pharisees noted about Jesus' ministry was His authority. They said His words were spoken with authority (Matthew 7:29; Luke 4:36). He commanded evil spirits and they came out. Every believer has got some level of spiritual authority, but a five-fold minister has a higher level of authority that is not available to all believers. And they are all unique. The authority Paul had was different from that of Peter. Both were apostles, but the operation of their gifts as apostles was different. Peter was called to the Jews, but Paul was called to the Gentiles.

Passion for Equipping the Saints for Ministry

Every believer who has a gift of healing, or prophecy, or other gifts will exercise that gift wherever they go to serve the body as the Holy Spirit leads them. Their main goal is to bless others with the gifts they have. A five-fold minister's perspective is not the same. Their heart's desire is to help others find their gifts and their function, and reach their potential. Their dream is to see others discover their purpose and grow in the Lord and be equipped to do the work they have been assigned by God. They are always trying to help people get to the next level. Sometimes it is hard to be around these people because they will challenge you to grow up and will not be satisfied with where you are right now.

When a five-fold minister sees a believer, they see what they could become if they did this, this, and this. They are not willing to accept their current situation as final; they will always see room for growth and development. A five-fold minister has the ability to recognize the hidden potential in a believer and help that believer manifest that potential.

Unity of the Body of Christ

Another trait of five-fold ministry is a passion for the unity of the saints, regardless of denominational or cultural barriers. They will always work for the benefit of the whole body of Christ. They will have a larger perspective about what God is doing on this earth, rather than a limited vision for only their own church or ministry. If they are true ministers of the gospel, they will work for the unity of the body. There are false apostles and false prophets (2 Corinthians 11:13). These false ministers will have no heart for the unity of the body; the motivation behind their ministry is their own belly (Romans 16:18). A true apostle focuses on the big picture and listens to God's orders for the body of Christ.

Unusual Revelation of the Word and God

Those who are called into five-fold ministry will have a revelation of the Word and of God that a normal believer will not have. They are called to teach and preach the Word, which means they must have an in-depth knowledge of the Word. They will have the capacity to know more than an average believer knows. They will have a hunger to learn and grow in the things of God. When the people heard the apostles in the book of Acts, they were astonished at their teaching (Acts 4:13).

Manifestation of the Gifts of the Spirit

Though the manifestation of the gifts of the Spirit is not a sign for five-fold ministry, if you are called to five-fold ministry there should be manifestations of the gifts of the Spirit in you. Of course, everyone may not manifest the same gifts. We need to be happy with whatever the Holy Spirit gives us, and then desire and ask for the gifts we would like to have.

A Pure Motivation to Glorify God in All They Do

When you are called to five-fold ministry, you have an inborn desire to see God's kingdom extended and established on the earth. That is one of the signs of a genuine call of God. Your whole life's motivation is to see God's name glorified and people's lives changed and impacted.

Extraordinary Passion

A five-fold minister is sold out for God. They eat, sleep, and breathe their calling and the thing he or she cares about the most is to fulfill that call. They will sacrifice anything to be in the center of His will because a true five-fold minister is a direct extension of Jesus Christ here on earth. They live an intense life and feel the burden for the whole world. They are always curious about what is going on in the earth. They have a passion for God, souls, and the kingdom of God more than others. They are naturally passionate people and they cannot separate themselves from the call they have. They often feel lonely. They are what they are called to be.

Supernatural Provision from God

If God called you into five-fold ministry or to accomplish any of His purposes, it is His responsibility to provide for you. If He is not providing for you to do what you feel He has called you to do, He has either not called you to do it or it is not His time yet. *Your provision is in your purpose.* The spiritual inheritance you received as a child of God includes everything you need to fulfill your purpose.

Worldwide Perspective

A person who is called into five-fold ministry will have a global perspective on what God is doing. There are some five-fold ministers who are called to raise up local bodies of believers in cities or regions so he or she may not travel all over the world—but they will have a heart for the whole world because that is the heart of God. They have an ability to fit into any culture or language and be in a foreign country and feel right at home.

Extra Measure of Faith

The Bible says each of us is given a measure of faith according to the measure of Christ. Each of us has received faith to the level we need to fulfill our purpose. Five-fold ministers need an extra measure of faith to fulfill their call. All of the ministry, miracles, mighty works, or any accomplishment God does through them, come through that faith they have received from God.

Supernatural Upbringing

Those who are called to five-fold ministry are chosen by God and created by God for that purpose. God makes the choice. The individual has nothing to do with it. They do not get to choose what they would like to do, but they can rebel and disobey the call. God will create them in a way that He will put the desire, call, and the anointing in them and divinely guide them to reach that place of ministry. When God calls them through any event, they will have an inner sense or a sudden realization of their destiny. If we study the lives of people God used in five-fold ministry, almost all of them will say they were planning to do something different but God called them to be His minister.

There is an element of supernatural phenomena involved in these people's lives. From the time they are born, there will be incidents and events that lead them to reach the place of their calling. The enemy targets them to destroy their lives, but nothing can annul what God has purposed. My desire was to be an electronic engineer. But when God's call came knocking at the door, it bore witness with my spirit and I surrendered to that call.

They Are the Gift to the Body of Christ

One of the main differences between a believer who has the gifts of the Holy Spirit and a five-fold ministry gift is a believer *has* a gift of the Holy Spirit, but the one who is called to the five-fold ministry *is* the gift. That means the one who is called to the apostolic ministry does not possess the *gift* of an apostle. Instead he or she *is* the gift of apostle to the body of Christ. A person who has the gift of prophecy is not necessarily a prophet. He might be a salesman by profession, and possess a gift of prophecy from the Holy Spirit. The one with the five-fold call is a prophet and is a gift to the body of Christ.

They May Begin Something New That Was Never Seen Before

Because God gives these people a unique revelation of Him and His Word, which is not widely known or was never known before, He uses them to do something (or they may do things in a way) that was never seen before. It is their desire to teach and share their revelation so that all people will know that truth and benefit from it. Sometimes it's the beginning of a new movement. We see this in the lives of Noah, Abraham, Moses, and Paul. Noah built an ark and filled it with the people and animals of God's choice, thereby saving the human race; Abraham was called to leave his country to give birth to a new nation; Moses stood against the might of a nation to bring its slaves into freedom and then instituted the Law God gave him; Paul revealed God's directives for the New Testament church.

They Will Face Persecution and Rejection

Each five-fold ministry gift operates differently. They will have a different revelation, style, and way of doing things. Because their ministry and revelation are different from others, they will face persecution and rejection. Whenever something new is done in any society, there will be people who will oppose it. There are many reasons they oppose it. They have not heard God speaking this thing to them, so they may simply not understand it. They may be influenced by a religious spirit working through human tradition. There may be other reasons, too. Whatever the reason, this problem has eroded the unity of the church and caused many denominational splits.

A Secondary Call through Another Man or Woman of God

The call of God to five-fold ministry comes directly from God Himself. Later, God uses other ministers to confirm that call. We see this in the lives of Elijah and Elisha. God told Elijah to go and anoint Elisha as the next prophet. I believe Elisha already knew in his spirit what he was supposed to do and that is why he did not make any excuses. We do not see any evidence in the Bible that God spoke directly to Elisha prior to this. We see his call to the ministry of a prophet through Elijah. Elijah could not choose just anyone as his successor. He could not appoint his son or cousin, as we see today in ministries. God spoke to him about whom he should appoint.

Paul had an encounter with Jesus on the road to Damascus, but God sent Ananias to lay hands on Paul for him to receive his sight and the baptism of the Holy Spirit. Ananias was confirming what Jesus already called Paul to do.

We see the same in the New Testament church. As the early church grew, it also increased the responsibilities of the apostles. There were not enough people in leadership to take care of the needs of all the people. There arose complaints from the believers about unmet needs. The apostles selected seven men who were full of the Holy Spirit, faith, and wisdom, and they laid hands on them and appointed them for ministry. They were not preaching or teaching, but serving food and helping widows (Acts 6:1–6). Paul took Timothy as his protégé and trained him for ministry. Timothy's call was confirmed by the elders of the church (1 Timothy 4:14).

Paul and his team traveled through the cities where they started churches and appointed elders for ministry in every church. These are all people who were called by God through another minister. We will see such people in every church. Without them, the local church will not function effectively.

Unusual Training and Preparation

Those who are called to five-fold ministry will go through seasons of unusual circumstances and trials and preparation. There will be times when they will feel like they have been forgotten by God: even that they are going to die. God allows them to go through these tests to develop their character, faith, and trust in Him. If you want to know more about these tests and how to pass them, read my book, *Keys to Passing Your Spiritual Tests*.[8]

Bringing into Order What is Lacking

The five-fold ministry gifts are able to meet what is spiritually lacking in a person or a situation. When they are in a place or meet a person,

---

8 John, Abraham. *Keys to Passing Your Spiritual Test: Unlocking the Secrets to Your Spiritual Promotion.* Shippensburg, PA: Destiny Image, 2012.

they automatically recognize what needs to be done to reach the next level. They see things with the eyes of the spirit. They are anointed to put things together and bring the order of God into any given situation. Depending on their calling and spiritual jurisdiction, this could be done on a personal level, locally, nationally, or even on an international level.

Passion to Advance the Kingdom of God into New Territories

Because they are the gift and a direct representation of Jesus, they have a hunger to see God's kingdom advance into new territories. They will travel any length to preach and train others. Their heart beats with the heart of Jesus. They want to see souls saved and matured, nations rebuilt, and God's will done on earth as it is in heaven.

Unusual Opposition From the Enemy

The enemy knows and recognizes those who are called to five-fold ministry. They become his targets from birth. He will try anything in his capacity to destroy their lives, but he will not be successful. In their ministry they will also face tremendous opposition from the enemy, but the Lord will deliver them from all.

They Are Sold Out for Jesus Christ and His Kingdom

Five-fold ministers and their calling are very peculiar. They should be willing to walk away from anything at any time. Everything they have and possess should be at God's disposal. They can receive an order from heaven to move to the next assignment overnight. You do not negotiate when you receive that order. Remember the Macedonian call Paul received. That is the lifestyle of a five-fold ministry gift.

Responsibilities of a Five-Fold Ministry Gift

1. Equip the saints for the work of the ministry

2. Edify the body of Christ

3. Work for the unity of the body of Christ

4. Bring the body to the unity of the faith

5. Work toward unity in the knowledge of the Son of God

6. Mature the body of Christ

7. Bring the body to the fullness of Christ

8. Teach and establish the doctrines of the church

9. Appoint leadership and administrators in the local church

10. Exercise spiritual authority in the church and over the natural

11. Restore what is lacking in the faith of the believers

12. Show patience and longsuffering

13. Impart and stir up spiritual gifts

14. Share revelation and prophetic preaching and teaching

15. Establish churches and new ministries

16. Pioneer inventions and methods to advance the kingdom in the spirit and the natural

17. Bring together other ministries and ministers

18. Disciple others

19. Reveal the mysteries of the kingdom of God, the church, and Christ

20. Advance the kingdom of God into new territories

21. Bring to life the gifts and callings of God in others

22. Have a passion to bring restoration and healing to wounded ministers and saints

23. Sense the timing and seasons of God

24. Be an example in word and deed to the body of Christ

25. Reveal Christ and His kingdom to the world

Chapter 8

Apostolic Innovation

"It is God's privilege to conceal things and the king's privilege to discover them" – Proverbs 25:2 (NLT)

You might not have heard the term Apostolic Innovation. The Holy Spirit is a Spirit of Innovation. What is innovation? Innovation can be defined simply as a "new idea, device, or method."

When God decides to release something new on this earth, He releases an apostle. An apostle's job is to make the culture of the kingdom of heaven real on earth. The word *apostle* was used in the political world during Jesus' time. We know the meaning of the word apostle as a person who is sent, or sent one. But we have not been correctly informed about why this person was sent, who sent him, and for what purpose.

An apostle is a person who is sent by a government, king, or kingdom for a very specific purpose. They are sent when the sending authority wants a particular mission accomplished on their behalf. Their purpose is to accomplish the will and the mission of the sending authority in the country or the city to which they have been sent. An apostle's mission is multifaceted. Following are some of them:

1. To accomplish the mission and the will of the sending authority

2. Each apostle is sent for a very specific task

3. Their expenses and protection are guaranteed by the sending authority

4. Each apostle's mission and purpose is different from the others

5. To complete their mission in the window of time that is permitted

6. They are the representatives of the government or the kingdom that sent them

7. They are committed with their very life to accomplish the mission (in other words, it's a do-or-die situation)

When God releases an apostle, He releases him to reveal something new of Christ, the Church, the kingdom, or the earth that has never been revealed before. Otherwise, that person is not an apostle.

There are *apostles* in every sphere of life: science, technology, business, etc. When we lose touch with the element of innovation, we lose relevancy on this earth and in our culture. That is why the church is 150 years behind the world in everything. Many organizations, churches, and businesses that were once successful eventually died because they refused to change or update their system of operation. As a church, we are supposed to be moving with God in what He is doing at this day and time. Nobody wants to use the style, technologies, or systems used in the Sixties and Seventies in the twenty-first century. The world is changing faster than we think and realize.

What is innovation? Innovation is conceiving and delivering a cutting-edge idea, product, or solution to solve the most pressing need of our community and nation. What we call a miracle in the Bible is an innovation in the scientific world. A virgin giving birth to a son, dividing a sea without any equipment, a ninety-year-old woman giving birth, turning water into wine, interpreting or speaking in a language you never learned, are all examples of cutting-edge innovation.

When Pharaoh had a dream, he called all his soothsayers and magicians to interpret the dream but none of them could. He called all the educated and the most intellectual men of Egypt but they could not solve the issue. It was not known to man that a dream could be interpreted and God would communicate a world event through someone's dream, until Joseph showed up.

There was one man in Egypt upon whom was the Spirit of God: his name was Joseph. The Holy Spirit is the most innovative and creative Person in the universe. He gave Joseph the interpretation to Pharaoh's dream and changed the future and course of a nation. We are supposed to imitate Him here on earth.

There is a part of our brain that thinks innovatively, and in most people that part is lying dormant and is never activated. The time has come for the church to become the most innovative force. When we lose innovation and creativity we become irrelevant in society.

Pharaoh shared the dream with Joseph and the Holy Spirit gave Joseph the interpretation. That's innovation: coming up with a solution or a method to solve the most impending need of a nation. God was communicating to Pharaoh what was coming upon his nation through the dream. But it took the creativity of the Holy Spirit to figure out how to do it.

Every system and technology requires updates. When we don't update, we lose the most advanced features and functions of that system and technology. The church hasn't had an update for the last 500 years. We have been operating the same program and the same style for so many years, and we have lost relevancy. We became religious and lukewarm instead of innovative.

That's why people are not interested in coming to church. They have better things available in the world. The world and its children are very good in innovation. They think creatively while the children of the light sleep in the precious time God gave them.

Behold I do a *New Thing*

> "Behold, I will do a new thing, now it shall spring forth; shall you not know it? I will even make a road in the wilderness *and* rivers in the desert" (Isaiah 43:19).

The above verse might be one of the most innovative scriptures in the Bible. God says He will do a new thing. He will make a road in the wilderness and rivers in the desert. Just imagine with me how much innovation and creativity it will take to a build a highway in a wilderness or a desert and to create a river in the desert. He is always interested in doing new things in new ways. But because of the religious programming we inherited we think what we do is normal and Biblical. It might have been once but it has become outdated and useless now. We try to fit into the Bible what we do traditionally, which is wrong. We are supposed to change what we do to fit in with what God says in His Word.

We won't change or win the world through our shouting and singing. In the Bible, the people of God were ahead of the people in the world. God said that we would be the head. If you put an 'a' before the word 'head,' you will get the idea of how to become the head. You have to be a-head to become the head.

We should be ahead in knowledge because all the treasures of wisdom and knowledge are hidden in Christ (Colossians 2:3).

We should be ahead in economics because the glorious riches of His inheritance belong to us (Ephesians 1:18).

We should be ahead in education because we are the only group that knows the purpose of the creation of man (Genesis 1:26; Revelation 22:5).

We should be ahead in family life because God established the first family.

We should be ahead in innovation because the most creative Person lives inside of us (Colossians 1:27).

When we are ahead in an area of society, we will become the head.

May the Lord help the body of Christ worldwide to become everything He created us to be. May God use this book to bless you and release the spirit of innovation in you, in Jesus Christ's holy name.

Christ is the Chief Apostle. When God released Christ to the earth, He released something new: a new way of worship, a new way of relationship with God, a new way of living on earth, a new way to solve the problem of sin, a new way of walking in victory, etc. The Christians were known as the people of 'the Way' in the book of Acts (Acts 19:9).

Paul was an apostle. When God released him, a new way of relationship with the Gentile was open. Until then there was no way for Gentiles to come to God.

There are apostles in every field. Some are in the areas of technology, the medical field, science, etc.

Qualities of an Innovator

1. Able to understand the current trend

2. Able to discern the current time and season

3. Able to conceive something new

4. Able to think in a new way

5. Able to define a new way and new direction to the rest of humanity

6. Critical thinking

7. Creative problem solving

The last time the church had a system update was 500 years ago when the reformation took place through Martin Luther. Ever since we have had many different movements. Those movements are like different *apps* we buy and add to the existing operating system on our phone or computer.

When the prophetic movement happened, we just added that *app* to our existing program. The only thing we did differently was that we prophesied and trained others to prophesy and had longer services. When the holiness movement happened, everyone focused on holiness; when the faith and prosperity movements happened, everyone believed to be wealthy. It was the same with other movements. Now we have come to the season of the next system update. It's called *kingdom reformation* or the *kingdom movement*. Whether you are ready or not, this is the *next big thing* God is currently doing on the earth.

The specialty of the kingdom movement is that it involves everything. The kingdom of God encompasses every aspect of our life, society, and nation. Every doctrine mentioned in the Bible, every blessing and promise, is part of the kingdom movement. The only difference is this movement is focused on Christ and His kingdom and not on any human personality.

It's like the vision Daniel had of the rock that was cut out without hands, which struck the image and broke them into pieces. When Daniel interpreted Nebuchadnezzar's dream, he saw the toes of the image made partly of clay and partly of iron. Daniel 2:44 says that in the days of those kings God in heaven will set up a kingdom that will not be destroyed.

> "And in the days of these kings the God of heaven will set up a kingdom which shall never be destroyed; and the kingdom shall not be left to other people; it shall break in pieces and consume all these kingdoms, and it shall stand forever" (Daniel 2:44).

I found it necessary to say a few words on false apostles and ministers. In some parts of the world to which I travel, every minister I meet is an apostle, prophet, or a bishop. Just because someone uses the title won't make him or her a true minister.

Signs of a False Apostle or Minister

> "For such *are* false apostles, deceitful workers, transforming themselves into apostles of Christ. And no wonder! For Satan himself transforms himself into an angel of light. Therefore *it is* no great thing if his ministers also transform themselves into ministers of

righteousness, whose end will be according to their works" (2 Corinthians 11:13–15).

Is it possible for someone to come to one of our churches and preach a different Jesus than the Jesus in the Bible, and impart a different spirit than the Holy Spirit to the people—and believers gladly receive them? Paul says it is absolutely possible. Not only did he say it is possible, but he warned that it would happen.

> "For if he who comes preaches another Jesus whom we have not preached, or *if* you receive a different spirit which you have not received, or a different gospel which you have not accepted—you may well put up with it!" (2 Corinthians 11:4).

Let me tell you with a lot of pain in my heart that for a long time the church has been deceived by a different *Jesus,* and spirits other than the true Holy Spirit. The church has been hijacked by a religious spirit and the spirit of this world (please refer to my book, *Kingdom Secrets to Restoring Nations Back to God,* to find the signs of these two spirits). We did not even know or recognize it because everyone around us is deceived by the same spirits. How can we know the difference? I grew up in a Pentecostal church, deceived by the religious spirit for the first twenty-five years of my life. I did not know it because everyone around me was acting the same. I thought it was normal though in my heart I knew there was something wrong. *What I was doing did not sit well in my heart, but I did not know what it was.*

Paul warned the churches he established that after he leaves savage wolves will come to deceive them and to draw people after themselves instead of the Lord their true Shepherd.

> "For I know this, that after my departure savage wolves will come in among you, not sparing the flock. Also,

from among yourselves men will rise up, speaking perverse things, to draw away the disciples after themselves. Therefore watch, and remember that for three years I did not cease to warn everyone night and day with tears" (Acts 20:29–31).

These people who divided and continue to divide the body of Christ did not come from outside or from a different religion. They rose from within.

What they will do?

They Won't Spare the Flock

They will divide the believers into pieces. That's why we have so many groups of churches and no unity between us. We are all supposed to be one body, one flock, under one Lord and one Shepherd.

There was only one church in the city of Jerusalem during the life of the apostles. Each apostle did not steal a group of believers and start their own international ministry on the other side of the street. They could not even imagine doing such things. We have come so far from our roots! What we think and see as normal was not normal, and it was never supposed to be normal.

All the early apostles were part of one church in the city of Jerusalem. There was no Apostle Andrew International Ministries or James the Zealot's Holy Ghost Shouting Ministries. They were all part of one body. How was that possible? They were all more anointed than any of us are today. They had the power and gifts of the Holy Spirit flowing through them and they were all different in their personalities and personal preferences. Then how did they all work together as one? Peter's shadow healed people on the street. Their ambition did not motivate them to build something for their own name. They were one with Christ. Their heart beat for their Lord and Master who gave His life for them. Nothing else mattered to them. They were crucified to Christ and to this world.

I believe there is a way to have one church per city and all the needs of the believers' and ministers met. In the early church all the needs of the believers were met, and the apostles, elders, and ministers' needs were met as well. How did that happen? What kind of system did they employ?

When they received the anointing, the apostles did not branch out and start their own personal ministries. They all worked together as one body. It was as Jesus prayed: one flock under one Shepherd. That is the original plan of God for His church and still is in the 21st century.

They didn't divide the early Church into many pieces to meet each apostle's needs or ambitions. Today, I believe the number one reason for church division is personal ambition and to make a living. My request to believers and ministers is please don't use the church to meet your personal needs or to fulfill your personal ambition.

In New Testament times everyone did not go out and plant churches. Believers did not come up with an idea while having lunch together to start a new church. No. That's not the way things work in the kingdom. When Paul went around and started churches, he did not start ten churches in a city—just one. Each city had a church. Then one region had several churches.

In the book of Revelation, when messages to the seven churches in seven cities were given, they all start by addressing a single church, not churches. For example, "To the angel of the church of Ephesus write …" (Revelation 2:1). Then at the end it says, "He who has an ear, let him hear what the Spirit says to the churches" (Revelation 2:7a).

What would happen, and how blessed would it be today, if we had just one church in each city with all the believers united and working together to achieve the same goal? That would be the greatest miracle and a sign to the world that the Father has sent His Son Jesus to this earth (John 17:21).

It is the heart of God for such things to happen. I believe it will happen. The Lord did not permit me to start a church. Even though I wanted to and thought, 'That is what everyone else is doing; I should do the same.' When I look back now, I understand why the Lord held me back from starting a church in the U.S. If I had, I would have defeated the very purpose for which the Lord had called me. I would have added another faction to the existing wound instead of trying to heal it. If you feel the Lord is not releasing you to do certain things, know that there is a divine plan behind it. You might feel frustrated and angry because everyone around you seems to be doing what they want except you. Don't worry.

I also wanted to go on television, and let me tell you, I tried everything. I cried and fasted, but for some reason He hasn't let me do it. I noticed that people who began their ministries after me went into television and started doing crusades. I was so mad and upset, wondering, why not me? What's wrong with me? Maybe God did not love me enough. I struggled with all kinds of crazy thoughts like that. I wanted to start a training center, publishing house, etc.

Now, when I look back, I thank God for not letting me start any of those. If I had, it would have been a huge mistake, or premature births. I wasn't ready at that point. I did not have the message to preach. It would have been an Ishmael that I would have given birth to in the flesh. I would have built a little kingdom for Abraham John. How grateful I am to the Lord now for holding me back. I was not ready as a person and the message God wanted me to release through my life to the world was not ready yet. It takes a while to prepare a person to do what God has called, and then it takes another while to mature the message God wants us to release. Premature births can cause defects, physically and mentally.

Speak Perverse Things

False apostles or false five-fold ministers will speak the lies of the enemy to entice the people, promising them material benefits that will never manifest. At the end, believers will be disillusioned and abused. They may lose their purpose and life and end up dying disappointed. They will use every form of trickery and cunning craftiness of deceitful plotting (Ephesians 4:14).

If you listen to some of the things some so-called ministers speak today, you will have to cover your ears and mouth, wondering where they came up with their stuff!

Draw Away Disciples After Themselves

One of the major signs of a false apostle or a false five-fold minister is drawing people to themselves instead of the Lord. Their names will be more prominent than the Lord's name in their ministries. Everything will revolve around their personality and influence. They will treat others like slaves and sit on their throne expecting others to serve them. They want people to carry their Bibles and suitcases for them. They will name the ministries after their own names.

It's their own kingdom they are building and they use Jesus and His Word to accomplish their vision. That's why there is so much division among the body of Christ. Each leader will keep a group of believers to themselves and build an enterprise. Once they die their enterprise will crumble with them. Their goal is not to build God's kingdom or to accomplish His will on earth; instead, they try to accomplish their will using believers. Many are deceived—but this must stop!

What if believers worldwide were to unite and focus on building God's kingdom on earth? What if we were passionate about accomplishing His will on earth as it is in heaven? We could achieve this in no time. Not even a little demon would move its finger to do anything on this earth. They would run for the hills. Now, believers are running for their lives in many parts of the world.

If a person serves Christ wholeheartedly, Christ and His needs should be their number one priority. Christ wants His body to be united, not broken into a million pieces. That's His priority. All those who try to build a ministry after their names and personal ambition are operating contrary to the will of God. For a while they will shine, but the end will be pathetic.

> "Now I urge you, brethren, note those who cause divisions and offenses, contrary to the doctrine which you learned, and avoid them. For those who are such do not serve our Lord Jesus Christ, but their own belly, and by smooth words and flattering speech deceive the hearts of the simple" (Romans 16:17–18).

> "For many walk, of whom I have told you often, and now tell you even weeping, *that they are* the enemies of the cross of Christ: whose end *is* destruction, whose god *is their* belly, and *whose* glory *is* in their shame—who set their mind on earthly things" (Philippians 3:18–19).

Use Cunning and Crafty Words

> "That we should no longer be children, tossed to and fro and carried about with every wind of doctrine, by the

trickery of men, in the cunning craftiness of deceitful plotting" (Ephesians 4:14).

Another quality of a false apostle is using trickery, cunning, craftiness, and deceitful plotting. You should look up all those words!

It is time for the body of Christ worldwide to see what the enemy has been doing in our midst. We need to stop this as soon as possible. When that happens, we can evangelize the whole world. We can see nations coming to Christ in our lifetime. Nothing shall be impossible for us. May the Lord use this book to accomplish that purpose in Jesus Christ's Holy name. Amen.

Chapter 9

Believers' Areas of Ministry in the Church

"For in fact the body is not one member but many"
– 1 Corinthians 12:14

Jesus and the apostle Paul both mention some of the areas of ministry in which God will use a believer in a local church. This is not an exhaustive list; God can use a believer in any area He chooses at any time.

> "But the manifestation of the Spirit is given to **each one** for the profit *of all*: for to one is given the **word of wisdom** through the Spirit, to another the **word of knowledge** through the same Spirit, to another **faith** by the same Spirit, to another **gifts of healings** by the same Spirit, to another the **working of miracles**, to another **prophecy,** to another **discerning of spirits,** to another *different* **kinds of tongues**, to another the **interpretation of tongues**. But one and the same Spirit

works all these things, distributing to each one individually as He wills" (1 Corinthians 12:7–11).

"So we, *being* many, are one body in Christ, and individually members of one another. Having then gifts differing according to the grace that is given to us, *let us use them:* if **prophecy**, *let us prophesy* in proportion to our faith; or **ministry**, *let us use it* in *our* ministering; he who **teaches**, in teaching; he who **exhorts**, in exhortation; he who **gives**, with liberality; he who **leads**, with diligence; he who shows **mercy**, with cheerfulness" (Romans 12:5–8).

"*As each one has received a gift,* minister it to one another, as good *stewards* of the manifold grace of God" (1 Peter 4:10).

"And these signs will follow those who believe: In My name they will cast out demons; they will speak with new tongues; they will take up serpents; and if they drink anything deadly, it will by no means hurt them; they will lay hands on the sick, and they will recover" (Mark 16:17–18).

The last verse says those who believe cast out demons and pray for the sick. All believers are called to do that. Just because believers cast out demons and heal the sick does not mean they are apostles. We live in a day and age where people are attracted to gifts. As a result, we emphasize the gifts rather than character or calling. The reason for this is that very few believers discover their individual gifts. The majority of believers today are essentially pew warmers—they have no clue about what they are called to do or what their gifts are.

When someone in the body does discover and begin to flow in their spiritual gifts, others who have not yet found their own may admire them. They try to be like them and they begin to lust after their gifts too. Character and calling are not explored. Service to the body is not understood. People stumble and fall for lack of leadership.

Sometimes, when a person recognizes that he or she has a gift operating in their life, they leave their local church, start a ministry, and call themselves an apostle or a pastor. This should not be the case and could be avoided with discipleship.

> "And God has appointed these in the church: first apostles, second prophets, third teachers, after that miracles, then gifts of healings, helps, administrations, varieties of tongues" (1 Corinthians 12:28).

Today, the order outlined above is somewhat reversed. We give more importance to tongues, healing, and miracles than we do to apostles, prophets, and teachers. Paul does not mention pastors here, although he mentions teachers. We see in Paul's writings that it was the elders who did the teaching of the Word.

The word *administrations* is translated *governments* in the King James Version and other translations. There are people who have the gift to govern or lead the affairs of a local church. When a hundred people come together, they will have at least three hundred problems. Apostles cannot spend time with each one to solve their problems. They need the help of other mature believers who are able to handle such situations.

The Role of a Believer in a Local Church

The following verses are keys to understanding the function of a body, which causes the growth and edification of itself. As we learned before, the church is the body of Christ and a body is made of many members. Each member has a unique position and function, which enables the whole body to function properly. When one member of my body does not function properly, it affects my whole body. When one part of my body hurts, other members of the body reach out to help or bear the pain of the part that is suffering.

> "But, speaking the truth in love, may grow up in all things into Him who is the head—Christ—from whom the whole body, joined and knit together by what every joint supplies, according to the effective working by which every part does its share, causes growth of the body for the edifying of itself in love" (Ephesians 4:15–16).

All the members in my body are joined and knit together by bones, muscles, arteries, and veins. They are connected to my head. My hand is attached to my body and when my foot hurts, my head orders my hand to reach out to hold it to comfort it. If there is a cut on my foot, the hands cleanse it and apply the medicine that it needs. My hands do that entire job without complaining or asking for any special recognition or compensation from the foot or the rest of the body. The foot carries the weight of the whole body. Again, it does not have any special requirements for doing this.

That's the normal function of a body. If one of my eyes hurts, my hand is suddenly drawn to it to determine why it hurts. It will do everything it can to nurture and comfort that eye until it is restored. If the hand cannot fix the problem and it needs to be taken to a hospital, then my head will find further help and the whole body goes to the hospital to help that one member that is hurting. You cannot separate one part of the body from the others. That's why Paul says if one suffers, the whole body suffers.

> "And if one member suffers, all the members suffer with
> *it*; or if one member is honored, all the members rejoice

with *it*. Now you are the body of Christ, and members individually" (1 Corinthians 12:26–27).

When a church body functions in this way, it causes growth in that body and edifies itself. Because we are living in an individualistic society, it is very difficult to comprehend and apply these ideas today. It takes a radical change in our mindset to operate as the body that God intended.

If You are Saved You Have a Calling

If you are part of the body of Christ you are called by God. You cannot be part of the church if you are not called because *ekklesia* means called-out ones. Everyone is called to the body, but not everyone is called to five-fold ministry.

> "Moreover whom He predestined, *these He also called;* whom He called, these He also justified; and whom He justified, these He also glorified" (Romans 8:30).

> "Who has **saved us and called** *us* with a holy calling, not according to our works, but according to His own purpose and grace which was given to us in Christ Jesus before time began" (2 Timothy 1:9).

We should be sure of our calling and election as early as possible. We need to understand which member of the body we are and where we fit the best, so that we may not ever stumble or try to do something we are not called to do. Discovering our calling helps us find an entrance into the kingdom of God. When you discover God's kingdom you will discover your purpose as well. It's a simultaneous act.

> "Therefore, brethren, be even more diligent to make your call and election sure, for if you do these things you

will never stumble; for so an entrance will be supplied to you abundantly into the everlasting kingdom of our Lord and Savior Jesus Christ" (2 Peter 1:10–11).

This is not talking about going to heaven. You don't enter heaven by making sure of your calling, but by believing in Jesus. It's talking about entering and experiencing the kingdom here on earth. When you discover your purpose and function, the blessing of the kingdom of God will begin to manifest in your life.

You Have a Ministry

Every believer has a calling or ministry. They also have one or more natural gifts that God has given them. Though only a few are called into five-fold ministry, each believer is a king and a priest. As a king, you demonstrate and exercise your dominion over the natural realm. As a priest, you demonstrate and exercise your dominion over the spiritual realm. As a king, you use your trade to bring the spoils, the wealth of the world, into the kingdom. As a priest, you use your spiritual gifts to minister to God, to one another, and to bring souls into the kingdom.

> "But you are a chosen generation, a royal priesthood, a holy nation, His own special people, that you may proclaim the praises of Him who called you out of darkness into His marvelous light" (1 Peter 2:9).

> "And has made us kings and priests to His God and Father, to Him be glory and dominion forever and ever. Amen" (Revelation 1:6).

These Scriptures address every believer in Christ. In 1 Peter 2:9 the Greek word used for praise is *aretas,* which means "any excellence of a person (in body or mind) or of a thing, an eminent endowment, property or quality, a virtuous course of thought, feeling and action; virtue, moral goodness or any particular moral excellence, as modesty, purity."[9]

Any time you do something with a spirit of excellence you are *proclaiming* the praises of your God to the people around you, whether at home or the workplace. It is sad that many believe that our proclamation of His praise is done only through singing.

Very few are called to do ministry without using their trade or skill. It was not necessary for Paul to make tents to support his ministry: It was his personal decision to not become a financial burden on the people and churches to whom he was ministering. We see the opposite today where many ministers are accumulating personal wealth taken from their flocks. They milk their sheep until they bleed. I believe ministers should live well, but there must be a balance.

Some believers think that if a person is called into full-time ministry they should not do any other job or business. That is not biblical. If God specifically told you not to do any other job, then don't do it; otherwise God commands us to work with our own hands for our livelihood.

Four Different Types of Ministry of the Word

There are four different ways a minister preaches the Word of God.

> "But now, brethren, if I come to you speaking with tongues, what shall I profit you unless I speak to you either *by revelation, by knowledge, by prophesying,* or *by teaching*?" (1 Corinthians 14:6).

---

9 Thayer and Smith. "New Testament Greek Lexicon." #703. 151

Ministers will not minister the Word the same way all the time. We need to be careful not to fall into the trap of thinking that every time we stand up to preach the same thing should happen. If we expect that, we will become discouraged in ministry. We need to keep in tune with the Holy Spirit, listening to His direction about how He wants to move in a particular meeting.

The first way the Holy Spirit may minister His Word is through revelation or inspired preaching. He will unfold the truth of the Word in a way that we have never seen or heard preached before. It will be an apt word to the people who are present.

The second is by knowledge. It could be supernatural/revelation knowledge or knowledge learned by studying and reading. We will teach about parenting, marriage, how to manage your finances, church administration—all kinds of topics the body needs to understand—using the knowledge we have gained through experience and study. There may not be as much excitement and inspiration with this application.

The third is by prophesying, meaning we receive a word from the Lord about a situation, person, church, or a region and we release it just as He says it. Inspiration and revelation are included in that prophetic word.

The fourth is by teaching, meaning the Holy Spirit enlightens us about a particular subject to teach to the body of Christ. We break down the Word in a way that people can understand on their level. Teaching brings understanding about a particular subject.

Believers' Areas of Ministry to the World

Believers are not only called to use their spiritual gifts and minister within the local church but also to unbelievers. Every believer has at least one natural and spiritual gift. Remember the parable of the talents. God has given each person talents according to their ability and capacity. We need to develop our natural and spiritual gifts to be effective in our lives.

> "For we are His workmanship, created in Christ Jesus
> for *good works,* which God prepared beforehand that
> we should walk in them" (Ephesians 2:10).

This and many other Scriptures say that we are created to do good works. What is a good work? Any work that is done with excellence is a good work, but there is a hidden meaning in the above verse that we need to understand. Many view good works as doing something to help others, or charitable works. That is not what Paul meant by this phrase.

The phrase *good works* appears more than twenty times in the New Testament, especially in the letters of Paul. The Greek word used for *work* is *ergon,*[10] which means "business, employment, that which any one is occupied, that which one undertakes to do, enterprise, undertaking, any product whatever, anything accomplished by hand, art, industry, or mind, an act, deed, thing done: the idea of working is emphasized in opposition to that which is less than work."

When we develop and use our natural gifts and do things with excellence, this creates a platform for us to share the gospel with the people in the world. It is a better way to witness for God than simply preaching. That is why Jesus said in Matthew 5:16, "Let your light so shine before men, that they may see your *good works* and glorify your Father in heaven."

---

10 Strong, James. Strong's Exhaustive Concordance. Peabody, MA: Hendrickson Publishers, 2007. #G2041.

Our work is one of the ways we can show the world our heavenly Father. This could be through a business, product, service, talent, charity, or any enterprise we do with our hands or mind. When people see it, they should recognize our heavenly Father.

The doctrine of good works must be taught in our churches. In our efforts to preach grace we have neglected its teaching. As a result, we are focused on having fun. It is especially important that we teach our children about this because they are the next generation. In the first century, people did not go to church to have fun. They went to know and experience God and to learn how His kingdom worked. Then they went out and practiced what they were taught in every facet of their culture.

Every believer should master a trade or skill, form a business, and show to the world the creative and wonderful ability of our heavenly Father. Then we will not lack anything in our lives. When a need arises in the body, we will be able to meet that particular need. People will be standing in line to give when a need arises in the church.

There was a disciple in Joppa named Tabitha. She passed away from some kind of illness and the rest of the disciples were not willing to let her be buried, so they called for Peter to come and raise her up. One thing mentioned about this disciple was that she was full of good works and charitable deeds. She was so valuable to them that they wanted her back.

> "At Joppa there was a certain disciple named Tabitha, which is translated Dorcas. This woman was full of *good works* and *charitable deeds* which she did" (Acts 9:36).

There are two phrases used here: good works and charitable deeds. They are not the same. What were the good works Tabitha was doing? She made garments and tunics and ran a small business. From the money she made from the business, she did charitable deeds. This is an exemplary lifestyle that every believer around the world can emulate. Then we will not lack anything and the body of Christ will be productive.

> "Then Peter arose and went with them. When he had come, they brought him to the upper room. And all the widows stood by him weeping, *showing the tunics and garments which Dorcas had made* while she was with them" (Acts 9:39).

What an impact the church could make on the world if every body of believers developed and practiced both their natural and spiritual gifts! We could turn this world upside down.

> "Let him who stole steal no longer, but rather let him labor, **working with *his* hands** what is **good**, that he may have something to give him who has need" (Ephesians 4:28).

What would the reputation of the church be if the church had plenty, with enough left over to share with the people in the world, instead of waiting to receive something for free? Remember when Jesus multiplied the five loaves and two fishes and fed the five thousand? There were twelve baskets left over to share later. There is plenty for all in God's kingdom.

Now that we have learned what the church is all about and how it functions, let us move on to executing the purpose of the kingdom in our communities and nations. In the following pages, I will share about how a local church can execute kingdom purposes in their region.

Chapter 10

What Happened on the Cross

"Having disarmed principalities and powers, He made a
public spectacle of them, triumphing over them in it"
– Colossians 2:15

I strongly believe that by reading the previous volumes in the Kingdom Awareness series, you now have an idea about what God wants done on this earth, how His kingdom operates, and what the church is supposed to be doing. After reading this book, you will discover why most churches are not effective and why many believers feel disillusioned and disconnected from God and their life's purpose.

This book will enable you to understand why there is so little unity in the body of Christ and how various denominations, sects, and cults sprang out of it. God intended for His body to be one all over the world and to accomplish His will. God chose the people of Israel to do it, but they rejected the plan of God. I fear the church is doing the same.

After Jesus, the church should be the best thing that ever happened on earth. When we study the New Testament church and compare that with a present-day church, we see that we do almost everything opposite to how things were done then.

When you read some of these things, there will be many a-ha moments. What the Holy Spirit is trying to do is turn this huge ship, the worldwide body of Christ, in a different direction than it is going right now.

What Happened on the Cross

We know and have been preaching the forgiveness of sins that Jesus obtained on the cross for us. Jesus accomplished much more on the cross than just the forgiveness of sin. We are going to explore and find out what really happened. I don't have time or space to write everything that happened on the cross here, but I want to highlight something powerful that we have ignored and not preached or taught about much for a long time.

Jesus came to confront a kingdom, a kingdom that kept His children captive for more than four thousand years: the kingdom of darkness, whose king is Satan. Satan trapped us in sin, blinded our hearts and minds, and kept us under his dominion until the Messiah appeared. We were slaves to sin and Satan was our master. To free a captive or a slave, a ransom, or price, must be paid. The blood of Jesus was the ransom.

This kingdom of darkness was operating on earth and Jesus came with His kingdom to confront Satan. Certain requirements must be met by whoever is trying to deliver the captive. Satan is also called the prince of this world, or the god of this world. He was ruling this earth by keeping all of us his captives.

To capture a kingdom, you first need to defeat and capture, or kill, the king of that kingdom. Jesus Christ is the rightful Creator, owner, and heir of this earth. Satan is an illegal intruder. When the king is captured or defeated, it means that his kingdom is taken.

When Jesus was on this earth, He made some powerful statements that I never heard preached before. I am sure you might not have heard them, either. Here is the first.

> "Now is the judgment of this world; now the ruler of this world will be cast out" (John 12:31).

You can read that verse in any translation and find that the meaning is the same. Please read it one more time. The Messiah is saying, "Now is the judgment of this world; now the ruler of this world will be cast out." First of all, we need to know that Jesus is in the casting-out business, not the binding business as most Christians do and teach. When He said, *"now"*, when did he mean? Is He talking about something that is going to happen in the millennium, or is He talking about something that already happened two thousand years ago?

I hope you understand what you are reading. Based on this verse, this world was judged two thousand years ago and the ruler of this world, Satan, was cast out already. That means the ruler of this world, Satan, was cast out of his position two thousand years ago. If you do not believe that, let me give you another verse.

> "Nevertheless I tell you the truth. It is to your advantage that I go away; for if I do not go away, the Helper will not come to you; but if I depart, I will send Him to you. And when He has come, He will convict the world of sin, and of righteousness, and of judgment: of sin, because they do not believe in Me; of righteousness, because I go to My Father and you see Me no more; of judgment, *because the ruler of this world is judged"* (John 16:7–11).

The last part of the above verses says the judgment of the god of this world has already been done. If the ruler of this world is already judged and cast out, then why he is still acting like he is the ruler? I want you to think about this for a moment; I will come back to this.

Let me finish with what Jesus did on the cross and it will give you the answer to the above question. Jesus judged the ruler of this world and showed that he had no right to be a ruler any longer. To begin with, he had no legal evidence from the real Owner saying the Owner entrusted this earth and this world to him at any time. There was nothing, no evidence to show. He was keeping us all under deception.

If a highway patrol officer stops you, he will come to the window of your car and ask you for three things: your license, your registration, and your proof of insurance. The license gives you the right to drive a car in the United States. The registration proves you are the rightful owner of the car, and the insurance covers accidents or any other damage you might cause while driving the car.

Here comes Jesus the King with a capital 'K', the Creator and Owner of this earth and the world, to confront Satan because he has been claiming he is the god of this earth and that he has owned this earth and the people in it for a long time. Jesus stops him and asks him to produce evidence. The only evidence Satan can mumble out is the disobedience of Adam and Eve in the Garden. That is true, he deceived them and they fell. But the story does not end there. He asks Satan if he knows who Jesus is. Satan knows that He is the Son of the living God. But that is not all He is.

Jesus tells Satan that he deceived the first Adam and stole the earth from him, but He is another Adam, the last Adam who came to obey God in everything and take back everything he stole from the first Adam.

The greatest news is that you were in the last Adam when He confronted the devil and defeated him, just as you were in the first Adam when he was deceived, sinned, and disobeyed God.

Satan, as the ruler of this world, used his three most powerful forces to reign over us. They are sin, death, and the grave (or hell). Each of them produced different kinds of fruit in our lives. For example, sin produced poverty, curses, and sickness. I am going to walk you through this to show how our Lord and Savior Jesus destroyed all of these through His death.

> "Nevertheless *death reigned* from Adam to Moses, even over those who had not sinned according to the likeness of the transgression of Adam, who is a type of Him who was to come" (Romans 5:14).

> "For if by the one man's offense *death reigned* through the one, much more those who receive abundance of grace and of the gift of righteousness will reign in life through the One, Jesus Christ" (Romans 5:17).

> "So that as *sin reigned* in death, even so grace might reign through righteousness to eternal life through Jesus Christ our Lord" (Romans 5:21).

According to God's law, all souls that sin must die. The devil used one of God's laws, the law of sin, to keep us all under bondage. He cannot create anything new. Sin and death could only reign until the death of Jesus on the cross. Jesus introduced a new law to break the law of sin and death. It is called the law of the Spirit of life (Romans 8:2).

Jesus judged and cast out the ruler of this world. That means that legally, he has no right to be the ruler of this world anymore unless the children God put on this earth allow him. How long are we going to let him be the ruler? We (the church) decide. Then, on the cross, He took care of the other forces the devil used to reign over us: sin, death, and hell.

That is why Jesus had to become sin for us. On the cross, Jesus condemned sin in the flesh.

> "For what the law could not do in that it was weak through the flesh, God *did* by sending His own Son in the likeness of sinful flesh, on account of sin: He **condemned** sin in the flesh" (Romans 8:3).

Why did Jesus have to die? Why did Jesus have to become a human being? He had to experience sin and death, and then go to hell as a man. Only a man could become sin and experience death and hell for us because sin and death came to this earth through a man and the penalty of sin is death (Romans 5:12). If you have sinned, you must die. But by dying Jesus defeated death and destroyed him who had the power over death, that is the devil.

> "Inasmuch then as the children have partaken of flesh and blood, He Himself likewise shared in the same, that through death He might destroy him who had the power of death, that is, the devil, and release those who through fear of death were all their lifetime subject to bondage" (Hebrews 2:14–15).

> "But we see Jesus, who was made a little lower than the angels, for the suffering of death crowned with glory and honor, that He, by the grace of God, might taste death for everyone" (Hebrews 2:9).

These verses are powerful. They reveal the mysteries of why Jesus had to be born as a human being. He was made a little lower than angels for the suffering of death. If He was born as an angel He could not have died. You cannot kill an angel. They are spirit beings that live forever, whether they are good or fallen. Jesus became a man to taste death for all of us.

> "For since by man *came* death, by Man also *came* the resurrection of the dead. For as in Adam all die, even so in Christ all shall be made alive" (1 Corinthians 15:21–22).

If you are in Christ, you do not need to be afraid of death. Death and hell have no power over you. We can really face death and the grave and say:

> "'O Death, where *is* your sting?
> O Hades, where *is* your victory?'
> The sting of death *is* sin, and the strength of sin *is* the law.
> But thanks *be* to God, who gives us the victory through
> our Lord Jesus Christ" (1 Corinthians 15:55-57).

Once He died and rose again, Jesus said, "All authority has been given to Me in heaven and on earth" (Matthew 28:18).

Jesus defeated and destroyed Satan, but sin, death, and hell as well. There were other forces called principalities and powers ruling over nations. Let us see what Jesus did to those forces.

> "Having wiped out the handwriting of requirements
> that was against us, which was contrary to us. And He
> has taken it out of the way, having nailed it to the cross.
> Having disarmed principalities and powers, He made
> a public spectacle of them, triumphing over them in it"
> (Colossians 2:14–15).

If Jesus has received all authority, there is nothing left for anyone else. What did Jesus do after he received the authority? He gave that authority to His church, which is His body (Ephesians 1).

Not only that, but Jesus also gave us a kingdom and the keys of His kingdom to bind and to loose. Whatever *we* bind on this earth will be bound in heaven and whatever *we* loose on earth will be loosed in heaven. We are the ones who have the real authority and power now, not the devil.

Jesus went to hell for one reason: To take the keys of death and hell. He set free those the devil was keeping captive because of the law of sin and death. Every kingdom has keys, even the kingdom of darkness. He opened the door and let all the prisoners go free. If we do not have a kingdom, and the kingdom of heaven is not accessible to us, then why would Jesus give us the keys to His kingdom? Jesus came to give us back the kingdom, the whole earth. It belongs to Him but He gave it to us to manage for Him.

Positionally, we are exactly where we were before Adam fell because of Jesus. To be honest, we are in a better place than Adam was because we cannot fall like he did. How much of it is realized in the natural depends on the church. God has nothing left to do or undo.

Just as you inherited everything (your nature, character, attitude, position, etc.) from the first Adam through your natural birth, you inherit everything new from the last Adam when you are born again.

When Jesus was punished, we were in Him. When He was crucified, we were in Him (Romans 6:6; Galatians 2:20). When He was buried, we were buried with Him (Romans 6:4). When He rose again, we rose with Him (Colossians 2:12).

Now we are one with Christ. We have the same spirit, mind, and body (Romans 8:9; 1 Corinthians 2:16; 12:27). We are the body of Christ on earth. We are bone of His bone and flesh of His flesh (Ephesians 5:30). That is why the Bible says, "As He is, so are we in this world" (1 John 4:17).

"I *am* He who lives, and was dead, and behold, I am alive forevermore. Amen. And I have the **keys** of Hades and of Death" (Revelation 1:18).

Jesus defeated every force the devil used to keep us in bondage.

This revelation of the saints receiving a kingdom at the first coming of Jesus is in the book of Daniel. "But the saints of the Most High shall receive the kingdom, and possess the kingdom forever, even forever and ever" (Daniel 7:18).

When was the above verse fulfilled? If you read the context of the above verse, you will see that it happened at the first coming of our Lord because it talks about kings and kingdoms that were ruling on this earth at the time it took place. After the second coming of Christ, there won't arise any more kings or kingdoms on this earth. Now please read the verse in its context.

> " 'I, Daniel, was grieved in my spirit within *my* body, and the visions of my head troubled me. I came near to one of those who stood by, and asked him the truth of all this. So he told me and made known to me the interpretation of these things: "Those great beasts, which are four, *are* four kings *which* arise out of the earth. **But the saints of the Most High shall receive the kingdom, and possess the kingdom forever, even forever and ever**" ' " (Daniel 7:15–18).

It is important to read the whole chapter of Daniel 7. I have thought for a long time this chapter talks about the events that will take place after the second coming of Jesus. But recently while I was reading it the Holy Spirit illuminated my heart and I understood that everything mentioned in Daniel was not for after the second coming. There is so much revealed about what would take place at the first coming of the Messiah.

It clearly shows when the saints of God received His kingdom, and still many are waiting to die to enter the kingdom of God. What a loss! The incident where Jesus judged the world and the ruler of this world is told in Daniel hundreds of years before it took place.

> "Then I wished to know the truth about the fourth beast, which was different from all the others, exceedingly dreadful, *with* its teeth of iron and its nails of bronze, *which* devoured, broke in pieces, and trampled the residue with its feet; and the ten horns that *were* on its head, and the other *horn* which came up, before which three fell, namely, that horn which had eyes and a mouth which spoke pompous words, whose appearance *was* greater than his fellows. I was watching; and the same horn was making war against the saints, and prevailing against them, **until the Ancient of Days came, and a judgment was made *in favor* of the saints of the Most High, and the time came for the saints to possess the kingdom**" (Daniel 7:19–22).

The Ancient of Days came, and judgment was made in favor of the saints of the Most High God. When did this happen? Or is it talking about something that is going to happen in the millennium? This prophecy is already fulfilled. It happened when Jesus judged the ruler of this world and cast him out. From that time on is the time for the saints to possess the kingdom of God (Daniel 7:27). I will prove this to you from the Scriptures.

If you read the rest of the verses in that chapter you will understand it is talking about something that is already fulfilled, because after this judgment has been made there were still kings and kingdoms that arose on this earth. It cannot be in the millennium because there won't be any more kingdoms or kings that will rise while we are ruling with Christ on this earth.

Two thousand years ago, the Ancient of Days came and gave us His kingdom, but we did not possess it. We continue to let the enemy use most of the resources of the earth and rule over the people when he does not have any authority or right to do so.

At present, the enemy is like a criminal waiting for his or her final execution. He has been judged and sentenced, removed from his position and authority, and dethroned from his kingdom, but he is still acting like a king. Why? Because the one force that God put on this earth to keep him where he belongs is not doing its job. We are busy doing so many other things except what God put us here to do, and allowing the enemy to abuse, misuse, steal, kill, and destroy what belongs to our Father.

What has the church been doing so far? We have been acting and living like slaves, but full of pride, selfishness, and ignorance. We are letting a defeated ruler continue to rule the entire world. My Lord, what sad nonsense! We are so busy trying to get people to go to heaven we have been wasting the vast resources our Father has made available to us. Then we blame Him for not blessing us and meeting our needs. May the Ancient of Days open our eyes to see what is going on before it is too late.

When the eyes of our understanding open, we realize a few things. First, we will know the hope of God's calling on our lives. God has called you to do a specific task for Him in His kingdom, which is your purpose on this earth. Second, we will know what are the riches of the glory of His inheritance in the saints.

Once people understand their calling, the next thing they do is look for the resources to fulfill that calling. Your provision has already been added to your calling. All we need is a revelation of it. As children of God, you and I have received an inheritance. That inheritance includes everything we will ever need to fulfill what

God has called us to do. Our inheritance has riches that have been added to it. These are not normal riches, but His glorious riches.

Third, we will understand the exceeding greatness of God's power toward us, or that is made available to us. The power that has been made available to the church has no limit. It is exceedingly great. In other words, you cannot measure it. But we do not use even a fraction of it—only enough to heal some headaches and backaches. That is not all that Jesus gave us His power for. He gave us His power to administer His kingdom on this earth.

You might wonder why we are not able to use such power. There are various reasons and I will mention two of the major ones here. In the New Testament God did not give the power to an individual, but to His church. There are leaders in the body of Christ who think it was to them that God gave all the power. They are deceived. The second reason is that just because the Word says it does not mean it becomes ours automatically. We need to know how to receive it. That is what the next chapter is about.

We know and believe that God sent Jesus to die for our sins. Where did sin come from? Sin came because of Adam's disobedience. He lost the dominion over the earth and the rest of creation. Adam's sin affected us at six levels of relationship.

The Relationship Between God and Man

The Bible says Adam was the son of God. When he disobeyed, God came down to meet with him in the garden to reconcile. But Adam was not willing and hid from God. As I mentioned earlier, Adam carried the same DNA and the bloodline of God. He was created to do what God his Father does, which is to create and rule. Man lost the sonship and became a slave to his environment.

Through Jesus Christ, God decided to restore man to his original position. That is why John 1:12 says, "But as many as received Him, to them He gave the right to become children of God, to those who believe in His name."

Now we are sons of God on this earth. We are supposed to be doing what our Father is doing. He creates and rules. That is what we are supposed to be doing as well.

The Relationship Between Heaven and Earth

God's will was done in Eden as it was in heaven. There is no sickness in heaven, and there was no sickness in Eden. There is no poverty or lack in heaven, and there was no poverty or lack in Eden. When man committed sin, the relationship between heaven and earth was broken. Earth began to function without the favor and blessings of heaven.

Through Jesus Christ, God reconciled things in heaven and things on earth. Now there is no enmity between heaven and earth. This means that God's will can once again manifest on earth as it is in heaven. We need to believe this and act upon it. Again, we do not need to wait until the millennial reign for this to happen. If it were meant for the millennial reign, then God did not have to bring reconciliation between heaven and earth two thousand years ago.

The Relationship Between Man and Man

One of the major problems on this earth today is racial, caste, and tribal divisions. Humanity has been divided into thousands of groups based on color, culture, and languages, and they fight each other for dominance without understanding we all came from one man called Adam. When we have the revelation of the origin of mankind, instead of a limited scope based on our own little culture and environment, there will be peace among people groups and nations.

Jesus came with the ministry of reconciliation. There was enmity between the Jews and Gentiles, and He brought peace between them and created one new man (Ephesians 2:15). We have been given the ministry of reconciliation (2 Corinthians 5:18). Wherever the gospel of the kingdom of God is being preached, there should be reconciliation between races, languages, and cultures.

The Relationship Between Man and Nature

God created nature to serve man and his purpose. Because of man's sin, nature came under bondage. The enemy began to use nature against man to destroy him. Since the death of Jesus, everything that is under the bondage can be delivered and redeemed. That's why we need to preach the gospel to all creation, not just humans.

The Relationship Between Man and the Animal Kingdom

Humans and animals lived in peace before the fall. Sin affected that relationship as well. Since the reconciliation that took place on the cross, there are instances in many parts of the world in which wild animals and humans live in peace. If you search online you will be able to find them.

The Relationship Man Has With Himself

When God came down to the Garden to meet with Adam (after he committed sin), He couldn't find him. God called Adam, who he said he was hiding because he was afraid and because he was naked. God asked Adam who told him that he was naked? Ever since, there are two forces that keep men in bondage: Fear and nakedness. Naked means to feel inadequate and insecure, in himself and in his abilities. He does not feel qualified or worthy to do what God has called him to do. So he hides.

There are billions of men on earth today who have been in hiding. Inside, they are afraid and feel insecure. They are afraid to try anything new because they are concerned about what others will think of them. They are afraid to be genuine, authentic, original, and honest because they fear rejection. So they try to fit in with the crowd and remain a copy. They are afraid to fail and afraid of other people.

To cover that *nakedness,* men try to put on all kinds of suits and own all kinds of toys to feel they are important and to feel accepted by others. In my opinion, the majority of the things men do these days are to cover up that nakedness because they never took the time or the opportunity to deal with the insecurities and fears that have been hurting them for years.

I see men walk down the road with their hair colored like a bird and the waist of their jeans hangs below their bottom. Others have metal pierced all over their face and ears. They think they are being cool. All they are looking for is a little bit of recognition. They want to hear others say of them that what they are doing is cool, and it feeds their insecurities and ego.

These games are in every sphere of life. Some men talk about sports like they are the owner of a team when they can hardly throw a ball, let alone own anything. They are surviving on their credit cards.

When you come to church, you see those who do Pentecostal or Charismatic gymnastics during worship. Many of them want others to think they are so spiritual and in the third heaven, walking with Jesus shoulder to shoulder.

God in Christ Jesus restored our search for significance. He accepted us in the beloved before the foundation of the world (Ephesians 1:3–6).

Reconciliation took place through the cross in the following areas.

God and Man were Reconciled

"For if when we were enemies we were reconciled to God through the death of His Son, much more, having been reconciled, we shall be saved by His life" (Romans 5:10).

"And you, who once were alienated and enemies in your mind by wicked works, yet now He has reconciled" (Colossians 1:21).

The relationship between man and God was broken because of sin. Through the shed blood of Jesus and His death on the cross, the relationship between man and God was restored.

Things in Heaven and Things on Earth Were Reconciled

"That in the dispensation of the fullness of the times He might gather together in one all things in Christ, both which are in heaven and which are on earth—in Him" (Ephesians 1:10).

"And by Him to reconcile all things to Himself, by Him, whether things on earth or things in heaven, having made peace through the blood of His cross" (Colossians 1:20).

Heaven and earth were not in alignment since the fall of man. Through His death on the cross, things in heaven and things on earth were reconciled and brought into total alignment. Now what is in heaven can manifest on earth.

The same life that is in heaven can manifest on earth. We need to believe this and appropriate it into every area of our life on earth.

Jews and Gentiles were Reconciled

"Therefore remember that you, once Gentiles in the flesh—who are called Uncircumcision by what is called the Circumcision made in the flesh by hands— that at that time you were without Christ, being aliens from the commonwealth of Israel and strangers from the covenants of promise, having no hope and without God in the world. But now in Christ Jesus you who once were far off have been brought near by the blood of Christ.

"For He Himself is our peace, who has made both one, and has broken down the middle wall of separation, having abolished in His flesh the enmity, *that is,* the law of commandments *contained* in ordinances, so as to create in Himself one new man *from* the two, *thus* making peace, and that He might reconcile them both to God in one body through the cross, thereby putting to death the enmity. And He came and preached peace to you who were afar off and to those who were near. For through Him we both have access by one Spirit to the Father" (Ephesians 2:11–18).

God brought down the racial pride of the Jews who thought they were the best race in the world and that everyone was under them.

The Bible does not teach such a message. They were great based on their obedience to their God, not based on their race. When they disobeyed their God, they were sold as slaves. The Jews might have been in slavery and in captivity more than any other race on this earth.

It is sad today that many believers in Christ think that somehow they do not measure up to the same level as a Jewish person. Others are afraid to speak the truth for fear of anti-Semitism or Replacement Theology. I do not believe in Replacement Theology either, but because they rejected God and His covenant, God decided to extend the same covenantal blessings, promises, favor, and protection to the Gentiles through Jesus Christ. I call it the Extended Theology. We are supposed to be on this earth what the Israelites were in the Old Testament, and more.

When Jesus talked about John the Baptist, He said there is not a man who was born of women that is greater than John the Baptist. Then He said that he who is least in the kingdom of God is greater than John the Baptist.

> "Assuredly, I say to you, among those born of women
> there has not risen one greater than John the Baptist;
> but he who is least in the kingdom of heaven is greater
> than he" (Matthew 11:11).

John the Baptist was a Jew and he was the greatest among those born of women, but according to Jesus the one who is least in the kingdom of heaven is greater than John the Baptist. You and I are greater than John the Baptist.

Don't let anyone ever convince you that God did not bless you with the same blessings as the Jews. They are the children of God and so are we (John 1:12). They are the seed of Abraham and so are we

(Galatians 3:29). They are a chosen people and so are we (Ephesians 1:3 and 1 Peter 2:9). They inherited the promise of Abraham and so did we (Galatians 3:29). They are a kingdom of priests and so are we (1 Peter 2:9). They are the heirs of God and so are we (Romans 8:17). We are grafted into the same blessings and promises God gave to the Jews. These are all done and received by faith and not by keeping any Jewish traditions.

I have heard many prominent ministers and believers say the destiny of the United States depends on our support for the nation of Israel. They say that whenever America says or does anything against Israel, God will send judgment on our nation. I have a hard time digesting it for the following reasons. The United States was founded on July 4, 1776. Israel became a nation in 1948. There is a quite gap between the dates of the two nations' foundings. How can a country's destiny depend on another country that came into existence more than two hundred years later? By 1948, the USA was already a superpower in the world. How can anyone with any common sense say the destiny of America depends on its support for Israel?

Another misconception believers have is that if we do not bless or support Israel we will be cursed. The reason people say this is based on the Old Covenant. God dealt with other nations based on their treatment toward Israel. Germany and many other countries persecuted Jewish people, but today Germany is one of the most prosperous countries in Europe and the world is filled with German cars. Under the new covenant, God deals with the world based on their faith in Jesus Christ and what He has done on the cross, not how people treat the Jews. We are in the *acceptable year* of the Lord because of His grace and mercy toward us

The United States recently faced three of the most tragic natural calamities. Two big storms hit in Houston and Florida, and wildfires still burn in California as I write this (2017). Billions of dollars' worth of damage has been caused by these disasters while the United States and Israel enjoy one of the most peaceful and close relationships in recent history. In fact, President Donald Trump made a visit to Israel since he took office as part of his first foreign mission.

America's destiny depends on one thing: The church (and the prayers of the saints in this country). Actually, Israel's destiny is dependent on the USA. If it weren't for this country, the Arab nations would have wiped Israel from the face of the earth years ago. There are more Jewish people in the United States than in Israel. Tel Aviv is known as the "Gay capital of the Middle East,"[11] and according to LGBT travelers it was ranked the "best gay city in the world" in 2011.[12]

Do you know who supports and finances the liberal and progressive agenda in the USA? Jewish businesspeople. The majority of the donors that sponsored the elections of liberal presidents in recent history in this country are Jewish. Israel is also the major recipient of foreign and military aid from the US government.

I am not against Israel or Jewish people. I am writing this to open the eyes of the believers in the United States. What I don't like is the way the enemy is using them to disrupt God's plan for this country. While you are supporting and singing about them, they are tearing down the moral foundation of this country. They are deceived by

---

11 Smith, Graham. "Tel Aviv Trumps New York to be Named World's Best Gay City." Posted January 24, 2012. http://www.dailymail.co.uk/news/article-2088319/Tel-Aviv-trumps-New-York-named-worlds-best-gay-city.html/. Accessed November 10, 2017.

12 Hartman, Ben. "Tel Aviv Named 'World's Best Gay City' for 2011." Posted January 11, 2012. http://www.jpost.com/LifeStyle/Tel-Aviv-named-worlds-best-gay-city-for-2011/. Accessed November 10, 2017.

the devil. My prayer for them is as the apostle Paul said in Romans 10:1, "Brethren, my heart's desire and prayer to God for Israel is that they may be saved."

Many misinformed believers around the world give millions of dollars to Jewish causes. Some of that money is being turned around and used against Christians and the church. That has to stop. If you do not believe what I wrote above, please research it and find it out for yourself.

Man and Creation were Reconciled

As I mentioned above, through Jesus' death on the cross things in heaven and things on earth were reconciled. Now God's will can be done on earth as it is in heaven.

Chapter 11

Receiving Spiritual Authority to Govern

"A man can receive nothing unless it has been given to him from heaven" – John 3:27

Nobody appoints himself or herself to an office of authority, either in the natural or in the spirit. Authority is always delegated because all authority comes from God. If anyone appoints himself or herself to an office of government, that position becomes invalid. It is just as true in the church. Just because someone thinks he or she would be a good pastor or a minister doesn't mean they should become one.

The spirit world is much more organized than we think. The demonic kingdom is organized and functions according to levels of authority. We read about their different ranks and positions in Ephesians 6.

Jesus said the kingdom of Satan is not divided (Matthew 12:26). If it were divided, it wouldn't stand. The reason the church is not effective is because of division. So many people appoint themselves and call themselves to positions of ministry just because they have a gift. The truth is everyone has a gift, but everyone is *not* called to a five-fold ministry position.

When we study the New Testament, we see that even those people who served food to the poor in the church needed to have hands laid on them and be appointed by the apostles (Acts 6:2–6). If believers who serve food need to be delegated with the laying on of hands, how much more every other service we do in church?

Regardless of what you are called to do, you need to be appointed to do it. Whether you are called to do business, to politics, arts, sports, being an usher, whatever: you need to be commissioned by an apostolic gift. I have seen good people suffer unnecessarily. They have a great vision, a plan, and the right knowledge, but they never get anywhere with that vision. They do not prosper in their business because of ignorance. They thought that because their calling is not *spiritual,* they do not need to be appointed. What about serving food? Is that a spiritual service? Whatever we do for God and His kingdom is spiritual.

The Bible says the whole world lies under the influence of the wicked one (1 John 5:19). He is acting as the god of this world right now. Before you go into the world to do anything for the kingdom of God, make sure you are commissioned to go and do it. It was after Jesus' resurrection that He told His disciples to go into all the world. He commissioned them to go. That was the secret to their success, not just the power of the Holy Spirit. There is a tendency among the body of Christ to believe that if they are baptized in the Holy Spirit they are free to do whatever they want to do. That is not the case in the Bible.

In the Old Testament, priests who killed animals needed to be anointed and appointed by their spiritual authority. The ceremonies in which they were appointed to their positions were very elaborate. It took serious preparation. Those who cleaned the utensils also needed to be delegated. So do not think your calling is exempt. The devil will use our pride and bring all kinds of excuses as to why we don't need to be appointed. Know that it is deception.

I believe that is the reason God gave me this chapter: To educate the body of Christ in how the ministries in our churches should operate. As the Bible says, everything must be done decently and in order (1 Corinthians 14:14).

Are you frustrated about praying and not seeing results? Have you been praying for your loved ones or certain circumstances or nations and not seeing things change for the better? I sense in my spirit that many of you have prayed and prayed for situations to change and almost lost faith in God and in His Word. It doesn't have to be that way.

We have heard teachings from the book of Daniel on how principalities and powers hindered the answer or kept the angel of God from coming to Daniel with the answer to his prayer (Daniel 10:13). That is an Old Testament example. In the New Testament, we read that Jesus disarmed the principalities and powers and made a public spectacle of them, triumphing over them and making them surrender their weapons (Colossians 2:15).

Though Jesus spoiled the principalities and powers, Satan still holds his kingdom together, and he is well organized in his operation. Both Jesus and God the Father acknowledge him, and he is authorized to do certain things until the appointed time. The devil cannot and will not touch someone without a point of entry. For him to be able to do something in a person's life, or in a nation, he has to somehow receive the right from humans to do it.

Now, the question is not *which* devil (or principalities and powers) is holding our answers, but *why* they are able to hinder our progress. It is always some form of sin and rebellion that gives place to the devil, whether in a person's life or over nations. When you have this revelation, you can recognize and receive spiritual authority from Jesus to destroy the works of the devil in your life and in the nations. Then, you will see more answers to your prayers than ever before. That is what this chapter is about.

Why, when a church declares certain things and tries to execute kingdom purposes over regions, does nothing seem to change? There have been so many declarations by so many ministries and individuals, but situations are not getting any better. When conferences take place, anointed ministers travel to certain regions and they decree and lead the church in corporate declarations into the spirit world, but again, nothing seems to change. I am really happy to answer that question.

The Holy Spirit began to show me why things do not change. There are certain spiritual principles that need to be applied if the change we declare is to take place. Just because someone declares something does not mean it will occur. If it were so, this world would have been destroyed a long time ago. It is similar to the difference between the authority of a citizen and that of a police officer. Though they both are citizens of the same country, they do not both possess the same authority. The police officer has the backing of a higher authority that the ordinary citizen does not have. Believe me: in the spirit, everyone is not equal and does not carry the same authority. In other words, the spirit world does not recognize everyone as being the same.

CHAPTER 11 | RECEIVING SPIRITUAL AUTHORITY TO GOVERN

Understanding Spiritual Authority

Before we can execute kingdom purposes over any region, we need to have a clear understanding about how authority works. God takes authority and our response to it very seriously. Lucifer became Satan because he engineered a coup in an attempt to usurp God's authority and he did not get a chance to repent. The first sin in the New Testament church was the rebellion that led Ananias and Sapphira to lie to the Holy Spirit, which led to their immediate deaths (Acts 5:1–9).

When the people of Israel were in the wilderness, any rebellion against the leadership appointed by God met with severe punishment. In the New Testament we read, "Let every soul be subject to the governing authorities. *For there is no authority except from God,* and the authorities that exist are appointed by God. Therefore whoever resists the authority resists the ordinance of God, and those who resist will bring judgment on themselves" (Romans 13:1-2).

Wow! It says there is no authority except from God. This applies whether to government, in the church, or in the family. Whoever resists or rebels against authority will bring judgment upon themselves. I do not think the Bible needs to be any clearer on the subject of authority. But when we look at the church today, many people operate without having much understanding about how authority works. They think that if they have a gun or a sword, they have the right to be a soldier. But owning a gun does not make you a soldier.

You need to receive proper training and receive authority from the proper channel before you can function as a soldier. It is the same in the body of Christ. Just because you own a Bible does not mean you are authorized to do everything it says, such as starting a church or trying to deal with principalities over a region.

We see this in the Bible with the seven sons of Sceva (a Jewish chief priest in the book of Acts), when they tried to cast demons

199   WWW.THEKINGDOMNETWORK.ORG

out of a person. Though they were the sons of a priest and used the name of Jesus, they did not receive any authority from King Jesus to deal with demons. I am sure that later on they were sorry for what they did.

> "Now God worked unusual miracles by the hands of Paul, so that even handkerchiefs or aprons were brought from his body to the sick, and the diseases left them and the evil spirits went out of them. Then some of the itinerant Jewish exorcists took it upon themselves to call the name of the Lord Jesus over those who had evil spirits, saying, 'We exorcise you by the Jesus whom Paul preaches.'
>
> "Also there were seven sons of Sceva, a Jewish chief priest, who did so. And the evil spirit answered and said, 'Jesus I know, and Paul I know; but who are you?' Then the man in whom the evil spirit was leaped on them, overpowered them, and prevailed against them, so that they fled out of that house naked and wounded" (Acts 19:11–16).

Everything God created and ordained works under some form of authority. The universe, marriage, church, government, children: Everything. The Bible teaches extensively about how these authority structures work. There is a specific reason for this. Everything God created works under the law of authority and submission. Nothing He created works on its own or independently. Everything is connected to, and dependent on, one another for its sustenance. That is God's will and plan.

If you think you are completely independent, just make a list of the people and places you depend on for your survival. You will quickly realize that the idea of being independent comes from the pride in our heart. And any form of pride comes from the very heart of Lucifer. Even when a person says, "I am proud of something," that pride is not of God. If we do well in anything, it is because of His grace and grace alone.

The majority of the things God created are made to *serve* and not to *lead*. Likewise, the majority of believers in a local church are called to the ministry of helps. We depend on oxygen for our survival. We may live without water and food for a few days, but not very long without oxygen. We depend on trees to produce that oxygen for us. Those are just a couple of examples of how dependent we are.

Just because you are a child of God does not mean you are authorized to change things in the spirit. When Jesus called His disciples to ministry, He gave them power and authority over sickness and demons (Luke 9:1). That means that until then, they did not have any authority over them, though they might have been brought up in a Jewish home. From that moment on, they were authorized to exercise that delegated authority over any sickness or demon. We don't read that they went through any healing school or had a three-week course in demonology.

The fight against demons and sickness is the base and ground-level operation of spiritual authority. Unfortunately, many believers tend to think that it is the greatest form of authority. He said that many would come at the end and tell Him that they prophesied, cast out demons, and did many wonders in His name, but He would tell them that He never knew them (Matthew 7:21–23).

It is very important to notice that the disciples did not receive authority over nations or governments, only sickness and demons. Some people take this verse as a general license to do anything they want. If you received only power and authority over sickness and demons, you cannot use it over governments. That's not the same authority.

In Jeremiah 1:10 and 51:20, we read that God gave Jeremiah authority over kings and kingdoms. These are examples of two different types of authority given to two groups of people by the same government or King. In the New Testament we see a similar principle. Peter was called to the Jews and Paul was called to the Gentile nations. They both received their authority from the same government and King, but they exercised it over different spheres.

Even in the natural there are different levels of authority. Every village or town has a government office and an officer who is authorized to administer or manage business transactions. When the state or district government appointed that officer and gave him that position, they appointed him to exercise that authority within a very specific boundary. He is authorized to operate only in that particular village. He does not have any authority in any other village. That does not mean he does not possess the capacity to function in more than one village. If he has the right qualifications, the state government can expand his jurisdiction or authorize him to exercise his authority beyond one village.

Being born in a particular village does not give you authority over that village, either; you need to be authorized by the local or state government. Many Christians tend to think that because they are born into the kingdom of God they have the right to do anything they want to do. That is not true. You need to be authorized by King Jesus to do anything in His kingdom.

The same principle applies in the spirit world. The spirit world is more orderly than the natural world. In the natural, you can manipulate certain rules based on who you are and who you know. This does not happen in the spirit world unless you come under the authority of someone who is already exercising authority in a particular region. A church or minister needs to receive his authority over different spheres and regions from the hand of Jesus.

Demonic forces are territorial. A demon cannot just operate anywhere because it wishes to do so. No, it can operate only in the area that is assigned by its overseers. We read in the Gospels that when a demon was cast out of a person it went through dry places seeking rest and found none. It could not just enter anyone it wanted or go to any place it liked. Finally, it decided to return to the same place or person in which it had previously dwelt (Matthew 12:43–44).

Another example is the demoniac in the land of the Gadarenes in Luke 8:26–38. This man was a wholesale dealership for demons. The demons begged Jesus, requesting where to send them. When the demons were cast out of this man, the people from the surrounding region asked Jesus to depart from their territory. Jesus had to obey because He had not yet received all authority in heaven and on earth to dispossess territorial spirits. When Jesus came the first time, He was authorized by heaven to exercise His authority in Israel only.

When Jesus was on the earth, He was authorized to operate in Israel. He did not go to India. It was only after He died and resurrected that He received all authority in heaven and on earth. He had to die and pay the price for all the sin of the world in order to receive this universal authority. Now there is no authority, power, or name above His.

> "It is the same way with these people who have entered your group. They are guided by dreams. They make themselves dirty with sin. They reject God's authority and say bad things against the glorious ones. Not even the archangel Michael did this. Michael argued with the devil about who would have the body of Moses. But Michael did not dare to condemn even the devil for his false accusations. Instead, Michael said, 'The Lord punish you!' But these people criticize things they don't understand. They do understand some things. But they

understand these things not by thinking, but by feeling, the way dumb animals understand things. And these are the things that destroy them" (Jude 8–10 ERV).

The above verses are powerful. The "glorious ones" denote angelic beings. The majority of the saints are not called to address Satan, principalities, or regional ruling powers. God did not give authority and power to an individual in the New Testament like He did in the Old Testament. He gave it to His church, and the church is more than one person. Two people can make up a church, so at least two people are required to execute any kingdom purposes. It is important to understand this.

It is a grave misunderstanding to think everyone is equal in position and calling. No. We are all equal in our relationship with God as His children, but there is a definite difference in calling and position. It's just like in a country, where each citizen carries different levels of authority based on their qualification and gifting. Jesus told His disciples that they would each sit on the throne with Him and judge the twelve tribes of Israel (Matthew 19:28). Everyone will not get to do that.

There are many scattered sheep in the body of Christ who are not connected to any spiritual authority structure. There are various reasons why they became scattered. They have taken the subject of authority lightly or rejected it and spoken against spiritual beings about which they have no knowledge as it says in the above verses. Or they were abused or mistreated by some people who were in spiritual authority. As a result, they have been robbed and constricted by the enemy. God wants to restore and bring them all back under proper spiritual authority so that they can function as He designed.

"*Then* the Lord knows how to deliver the godly out of temptations and to reserve the unjust under punishment for the day of judgment, and especially those who walk according to the flesh in the lust of uncleanness and despise authority. *They are* presumptuous, self-willed. They are not afraid to speak evil of dignitaries, whereas angels, who are greater in power and might, do not bring a reviling accusation against them before the Lord" (2 Peter 2:9–11).

Even though King Saul emotionally and physically abused David, David never raised his hand or voice against Saul. David understood the value of authority and how it worked. I am not saying people need to submit themselves to abusive leadership. Many cults and sects have done that and destroyed lives. What I am saying is if God appointed you to submit to a certain leadership like David did, then you must submit to that authority even if you may have to endure difficulty for a little while. You need to be careful about to whom you submit, and make sure that authority is appointed by God and not by manipulation, control, fear, or witchcraft.

> "Servants, *be* submissive to *your* masters with all fear, not only to the good and gentle, but also to the harsh. For this *is* commendable, if because of conscience toward God one endures grief, suffering wrongfully. For what credit *is it* if, when you are beaten for your faults, you take it patiently? But when you do good and suffer, if you take it patiently, this *is* commendable before God. For to this you were called, because Christ also suffered for us, leaving us an example, that you should follow His steps" (1 Peter 2:18–21).

These verses are not talking about some heathens in a remote village in Asia or Africa, but about people who call themselves Christians. They have lost the fear of God and live to fulfill the lust of their flesh.

If anyone operated in any form of authority in the Bible, they received it from someone. Though all authority is from God, He uses a human agency, whether spiritual or political, to delegate His authority to people. Jesus is the best example of someone who operated under proper authority. He did not do or speak anything on His own.

> "For I have not spoken on My own **authority**; but the Father who sent Me gave Me a command, what I should say and what I should speak" (John 12:49).

The devil told Jesus that if He worshiped him, he would give Him all authority. The devil knew that Jesus was the only person qualified to take authority away from him. He was offering Jesus a shortcut to receive that authority, but thank God, Jesus refused his offer and received all authority in heaven and on earth the way God had ordained.

> "And the devil said to Him, 'All this *authority* I will give You, and their glory; for *this* has been delivered to me, and I give it to whomever I wish' " (Luke 4:6).

It was through the death and resurrection of Jesus that He received all authority in heaven and on earth.

> "And Jesus came and spoke to them, saying, 'All *authority* has been given to Me in heaven and on earth" (Matthew 28:18).

The demonic kingdom functions under a proper authority structure. Though they lost all legal authority, demons are still trying to hold onto their kingdom. They are able to do so because of the support of human beings who are deceived and unknowingly give them the authority to continue to operate on earth. This state of affairs will remain until the church realizes what she has received.

Once the church begins to operate according to the plan of God, the demonic kingdom and its operation will begin to crumble city by city.

Even the apostle Paul acknowledged that he received his authority from the Lord and he received it through the local church leadership (Acts 13:1–3). But today, many believers do their own thing without any covering or protection of proper authority over them or their work. They end up as prey in the mouth of the enemy, and sooner or later they will have to run for their lives or will quit doing what they were called to do. They need to repent and get back on track because when people step outside of God's authority, He cannot protect them. They will bear the consequences of their actions.

> "For even if I should boast somewhat more about our *authority,* which the Lord gave us for edification and not for your destruction, I shall not be ashamed" (2 Corinthians 10:8).

> "Therefore I write these things being absent, lest being present I should use sharpness, according to *the authority which the Lord has given me* for edification and not for destruction" (2 Corinthians 13:10).

Even Paul said he ministered within the limits of his authority that was given to him.

> "We, on the other hand, will not boast beyond our proper limit, but [will keep] within the limits of our commission (territory, authority) which God has granted to us as a measure, which reaches *and* includes even you" (2 Corinthians 10:13 AMP).

The church is an army. Imagine an army trying to operate without any authority structure. Chaos would result. This army cannot win the battle because each soldier will try to do their own thing and get whipped by the enemy. God has appointed some authority structure in the church for its proper function, but because of abuses by some leaders, believers began to remove themselves from their place and from under any authority. This has to change if we are going to make an impact for Jesus.

The verse below shows the authority structure God has appointed for His church.

> "And God has appointed these in the church: first apostles, second prophets, third teachers, after that miracles, then gifts of healings, helps, administrations, varieties of tongues" (1 Corinthians 12:28).

Recognizing Spiritual Authority

When you confront the kingdom of darkness, it wants to know who gave you the authority you claim. That is why the religious leaders asked Jesus from whence He had received authority to do what He was doing. It was clear to all that Jesus had authority because He taught them as one who had authority.

> "For He taught them as one having authority, and not as the scribes" (Matthew 7:29).

> "Now when He came into the temple, the chief priests and the elders of the people confronted Him as He was teaching, and said, 'By what authority are You doing these things? And who gave You this authority?' " (Matthew 21:23).

The apostles faced the same question from the religious and political leaders of their time. They wanted to know from whence they had received the power to do what they were doing.

"And it came to pass, on the next day, that their rulers, elders, and scribes, as well as Annas the high priest, Caiaphas, John, and Alexander, and as many as were of the family of the high priest, were gathered together at Jerusalem. And when they had set them in the midst, they asked, 'By what power or by what name have you done this?' " (Acts 4:5–7).

Jesus was the Son of God and He had to receive authority to do what He did. Who do we think we are to operate without receiving authority, too? Certainly, we are not greater than our Master. He did not reply and say, "What do you mean? I am the Son of God and I have all the authority I need." No, He did not say that. Instead, he accepted their question as legitimate and wanted to answer it. To do that, He asked them another question.

There are no freelancers in the kingdom of God. In the kingdom, everything works within the proper authority structure. He asked them, "Where was John's baptism from?" Jesus had received the authority to do what He was doing through John's baptism.

Jesus is a king, prophet, and priest at the same time. From whom and how did Jesus receive the authority to be a king, prophet, and priest? You may say "From the Father," and that is true; but how, exactly? Jesus is a king, prophet, and priest eternally, but to operate on earth He had to receive these through the proper channels. Did you notice the genealogies in two of the gospels? That list is given to prove that Jesus is a king and the legal heir to the throne of David. That is how He received the right to be a king here on earth. He will sit on the throne of David (Luke 1:32).

How did Jesus receive the authority to be a prophet and priest on earth? Do you remember when Jesus said that the prophets and law were until John the Baptist? "For all the prophets and the law

KINGDOM GOVERNMENT

prophesied until John" (Matthew 11:13). According to Jesus, John the Baptist was the last prophet and priest (of the law) of the Old Testament.

We see in the Bible that when a king or a priest completes his assignment, he passes the mantle to another under God's direction either by the laying on of hands, pouring of anointing oil, or some other means. Jesus received the right to be a prophet and priest from John the Baptist. John was a prophet and priest at the same time. He was from the lineage of the Aaronic priesthood. Jesus had to be initiated into those offices, and that took place at the baptism service under John. John knew who Jesus was and was hesitant to baptize Jesus, but Jesus told him it had to be done to fulfill all righteousness. What righteousness? The righteous requirement of the Old Testament Law. Jesus was initiated into the offices of prophet and priest based on Old Testament requirements. That is the reason Jesus was baptized.

> "Then Jesus came from Galilee to John at the Jordan to be baptized by him. And John *tried to* prevent Him, saying, 'I need to be baptized by You, and are You coming to me?' But Jesus answered and said to him, 'Permit *it to be so* now, for thus it is fitting for us to fulfill all righteousness.' Then he allowed Him. When He had been baptized, Jesus came up immediately from the water; and behold, the heavens were opened to Him, and He saw the Spirit of God descending like a dove and alighting upon Him. And suddenly a voice *came* from heaven, saying, 'This is My beloved Son, in whom I am well pleased' " (Matthew 3:13–17).

In the Old Testament, when a priest was ordained into office he was washed with water, which represents baptism. Then a robe was put on him, and finally anointing oil was poured on his head. That is what happened in the Jordan River during Jesus' baptism. Baptism means to be washed. Jesus was washed in the Jordan, and when He rose from the water there came a voice from heaven, saying, "This is my beloved Son, in whom I am well pleased." That was the robe of righteousness Jesus received from His Father (Isaiah 61:10). Then the Holy Spirit came upon Him like a dove. That was the pouring of the anointing oil. I believe John also put his hands on Jesus, which transferred his prophetic office as well (Exodus 40:12–15).

Jesus did not only receive the Aaronic priesthood. He also received another type of priesthood, according to the order of Melchizedek (Hebrews 5:6,10; 6:20). The Aaronic priesthood is temporary, but priesthood according to Melchizedek is eternal.

Receiving Spiritual Authority Over the Gates of Hell

Now that you have an understanding about spiritual authority and how it works, let's see how we can receive spiritual authority to execute kingdom purposes in our lives and regions. Every town, city, and nation has gates of hell operating over and through it. Just because there is a mega church in a town does not mean the kingdom of darkness is going to be scared and pack up and leave. No, it will not. Whether it is a mega church or a small church does not matter.

Unless the church has a revelation and receives spiritual authority to legally forbid the gates of hell and its operation, the enemy will not give up. This is the reason most churches do not have much influence in the cities or towns in which they exist. When a church body receives revelation about the spiritual authority they possess, one can chase a thousand and two ten thousand (Deuteronomy 32:30). That is the proportion of how spiritual authority works in and through us.

The kingdom of darkness operates through seven gates on this earth. They are culture, religion, government, economy, education, media and entertainment, and science and technology. I have already explained this in detail in *The Power and Authority of the Church*. These gates are being occupied and controlled by the kingdom of darkness right now. The devil uses at least one of these gates to blind each unbeliever from seeing and receiving the glorious gospel of Jesus Christ.

Each believer is anointed and gifted by God to influence one or more of these gates at some level with the kingdom of God. That is our kingdom assignment. God has put a divine passion in each of us to reach these specific areas. We need to discover our gifts and develop and use them to influence the community in which we are living. Each believer can receive authority over the particular area they feel they are called to influence and take it as an assignment to pray over that sphere specifically.

Each of these gates has different demonic entities that rule over and through them. Before we address any of these gates in prayer, we need to make sure we receive authority over those gates, and the spiritual forces behind them, from Jesus Christ. Either that or we must find an apostle who has revelation about this and bring him into your area to train, minister, and deal with those gates: To lay hands and appoint local believers to do it.

One of the main reasons Jesus started His church is to forbid the gates of hell from executing their purposes on earth (Matthew 16:18). Knowing this, the church that is operating in a town needs to go to Jesus and receive authority over the spirit world first. Then over businesses, government, the education system, the economy, and other spheres through which the gates of hell are operating in that region, because the whole world lies under the influence of Satan (1 John 5:19).

Most churches think that if they take more people to heaven, they are doing them and God a favor. Or if we worship long enough, the powers of darkness will leave town. Not necessarily. Our mission is not to populate heaven. Our mission is to help the Father and the Son accomplish their mission on earth. This job is two-faceted. Our Father wants the enemies of His Son brought to His footstool in submission. The Son wants to submit all the kingdoms of this earth back to the Father (1 Corinthians 15:24; Revelation 11:15).

Even Paul had to receive the authority to do what he was called to do. Just because he was called did not give him the authority to go and deal with demonic entities that ruled regions. He had to be commissioned by the laying on of hands, by the church. This happened at Antioch.

While the church was fasting and praying, the Holy Spirit said, "Now separate to Me Barnabas and Saul for the work to which I have called them" (Acts 13:2b). The whole church fasted and prayed and laid hands on them, and then they sent them away.

The next verse says, "So being sent out by the Holy Spirit" (Acts 13:3a). It was the Holy Spirit who sent them out, but He used the church as the agency to do it. That is the purpose of the church: To work as an agency for the Holy Spirit to do what He wants to do.

How do we receive authority over the gates of hell ruling in a region? Make sure you are properly placed under the spiritual authority of a five-fold ministry gift. Do not be a freelancer and then go and try to deal with hell. You may experience what the sons of Sceva experienced. This is true for individuals and churches.

Every church in the New Testament was under an apostolic covering; most of them were established by Paul and were under his authority. After his death, all of those great churches eventually disappeared from the face of the earth because the believers failed to continue the system he established.

Paul prophesied after his death that false teachers and prophets would rise from among them. He called these false prophets and teachers *savage wolves* (Acts 20:29). The reason hundreds of churches are closing their doors every year is because they do not understand spiritual authority and they do not place themselves under proper spiritual authority. When they think of church, they think it's like starting a franchise of a fast food chain.

Make sure the devil and his kingdom have no legal right over your life. Make sure you are not harboring hatred, bitterness, offences, unforgiveness, or sin toward anyone in your heart, and that you do not have anything that belongs to the enemy. As Paul said 2 Corinthians 10:6, "And being ready to punish all disobedience when your obedience is fulfilled." That means before you go to exercise authority over demons, make sure you are walking in obedience to God.

Once your obedience is complete, you need to go to the court of heaven in the spirit, trusting the blood of Jesus to clear anything the enemy is accusing you of before the throne of God. Believe it or not, everyone has something that the enemy is using to accuse them. He is called the accuser of the brethren. How does a person do that practically? I would encourage you to listen to the messages online about the court of heaven.

Any area of your life that you have not been able to live in accordance with God's Word gives the enemy a legal right to withhold that blessing from manifesting in your life. If you have prayed and prayed about an area for years and have not seen any changes or breakthroughs, the enemy has a legal hold there. He received the right to interfere in your life. Please know that God is for you and He will not withhold anything good from those that walk uprightly

(Psalm 84:11; Romans 8:31). You need to go to God's courtroom to address those issues, just like you do in the natural. The court in heaven works just like the one in the natural. The only difference is that it is based on justice, righteousness, and truth.

To go to court in heaven, you pray, saying, "Heavenly Father, I come into your court through the blood of Jesus and ask You to show me the reason I am not seeing a breakthrough (mention any particular area you are struggling in) and forgive me for any sins I or my forefathers have committed against you, which gave the devil a legal right to access that area of my life. Thank You for forgiving me and my forefathers." Now, believing that you received the forgiveness, you address your accusers by saying, "I cancel every accusation and legal right the enemy has over (say that area) by the blood of Jesus. I command the enemy to restore everything he has stolen (say that particular area of your life) in Jesus Christ's holy name."

How Do You Receive Spiritual Authority?

Nothing happens automatically in the kingdom. Salvation, healing, forgiveness, and everything else must be received by faith. The same goes with receiving authority. An ekklesia receives spiritual authority over the gates of hell by asking through prayer.

> "Ask, and it will be given to you; seek, and you will find; knock, and it will be opened to you. For everyone who asks receives, and he who seeks finds, and to him who knocks it will be opened" (Matthew 7:7–8).

> "Ask of Me, and I will give *You* the nations *for* Your inheritance, and the ends of the earth *for* Your possession" (Psalm 2:8).

If you do not ask, you do not receive nations as your possession and the ends of the earth as your inheritance. If you are receiving authority over a particular government as a church, you say, "We receive authority over the government of (mention the region or nation) from the hands of Jesus Christ to execute, legislate, and administer God's kingdom purposes." Then you listen to the Holy Spirit to hear anything else He says and do it accordingly. He is the Governor. After you pray, believe you received the authority. Pray in like manner to receive authority over each gate of hell previously mentioned. Then use that authority to stop, cancel, and forbid the enemy's operation through those gates. Now you are functioning as one who received authority to administer God's kingdom.

An ekklesia needs to receive authority not only over the gates of hell, but over every aspect of creation that is created by God. God has created man to have dominion over everything He has created. Please read Psalm 8:4–6, which says, "What is man that You are mindful of him, and the son of man that You visit him? for You have made him a little lower than the angels, and You have crowned him with glory and honor. You have made him to have dominion over the works of Your hands. You have put all *things* under his feet."

We must do this because the enemy can use any medium to fight against us. So receive authority over water, air, fire, the animal kingdom, vegetation, solar system, weather, etc., and command everything to line up with God's Word and to work as God intended (Psalm 121:5–8). Remember, Joshua commanded the sun and moon to obey (Joshua 10:12–13).

Before you pray over any issues in your community or nation, first receive authority over that community and nation in the spirit and then pray. To receive authority, you say, "In the name of Jesus, I/ we receive spiritual authority over _____ to exercise spiritual juris-diction." Without receiving authority, you can fast all you want and declare anything, but nothing will change. But if you have authority, you just say it once.

"Thou shalt also decree a thing, and it shall be established unto thee: and the light shall shine upon thy ways" (Job 22:28 KJV).

If all that was required for people to exercise spiritual authority was to believe and use the name of Jesus, then it would have worked for the sons of Sceva. Unfortunately, that was not enough even though they were the sons of a priest. The sons of Sceva did not get registered on the list the demons had of the people who had obtained authority over them. How about you?

There are people to whom God gives authority as part of their call. Apostles, prophets, and evangelists are the ones who receive this as part of their calling. Their job is to train the church to receive and exercise God-given authority. It is dangerous to assume you have received this authority when you have not. Or to assume you are called into a ministry because you like what someone else is doing.

Receiving authority is like receiving salvation. Though Jesus paid the price for the sin of the world, not everyone is saved. Why? Because not everyone knows about it and submits to it. Each person needs to believe and appropriate it into their lives. It is the same with authority.

The kingdom of God rules over the kingdoms of men. God told Moses He had made him as God over Pharaoh and all the land of Egypt (Exodus 7:1). Whatever he said over the land of Egypt would happen. And it did.

Exercising Spiritual Authority

Once you receive spiritual authority, it does not mean you can use it as you wish. It must be used wisely and as directed by the Holy Spirit, otherwise you will destroy yourself and others. Please read the verses below.

"For even if I should boast somewhat more about *our authority*, which the Lord gave us for edification and not for your destruction, I shall not be ashamed" (2 Corinthians 10:8).

"Therefore I write these things being absent, lest being present I should use sharpness, according to *the authority which the Lord has given me* for edification and not for destruction" (2 Corinthians 13:10).

Paul said he used the authority he received for edification and not for destruction. One of the reasons God holds back authority from people is if He knows they will use it for another's destruction. You have only one enemy, the devil. God's authority must never be used against people, but only against the spiritual forces that are working through people. Declare people as innocent: Whatever evil they do, they do out of ignorance and deception.

Though Jesus received authority, He only used it as directed by the Holy Spirit. He said the Son could do or speak nothing on His own. Imagine the total trust He had to have in the Holy Spirit and the Father. Each of us needs to come to that place of total surrender and dependency on God for everything. Until then, this authority will not work effectively in and through us. God knows it will bring harm rather than benefit to us if we are not properly submitted and dependent on Him.

What does it take to legislate something in the spirit? How do we legislate? It takes a minimum of two people to come into agreement concerning anything to legislate something on behalf of the kingdom of God. Our King has sanctioned us by saying that if two of us agree on earth and ask anything in His name, He will do it (Matthew 18:19). We cannot have any more sure promise than that. What if the president of the United States gave us a promise, in writing, saying that when two of us come to him in agreement concerning anything, he will approve that request and issue an order to carry it out? I think we would believe it because we have it in writing with his signature. How much more should we believe our Lord Jesus Christ when He gives us a promise?

God's desire is to see His will done *on earth as it is in heaven*. He has put His church, the governing body of His kingdom, on earth to realize that plan. It is done is like this: When you see something that is not in alignment with His kingdom, the church receives a revelation of how it is in heaven and brings that situation or area in alignment with heaven through prayer and proper action.

It does not require much effort to find something here that is not in alignment with heaven. We need to start with our personal lives and bring our lives in tune with God's kingdom and His purposes. Then we are able to go out and change the world. First, we need to discover His kingdom, receive a revelation of how it operates, and live in it personally. Then we can tell others who are outside the kingdom. In today's culture, the church has been dependent on the world for everything. They have no idea what God's kingdom is or how it operates. They have been told they will go to heaven when they die, and that's about it. That is not the way the early church taught its believers. They did not preach a gospel that scared people about hell so they would go to heaven. Most believers are waiting to get raptured out of here because of this. We have been taught wrong.

Spiritual Jurisdiction

When we receive spiritual authority, we cannot use it anywhere for anything we wish. God gives us the authority to accomplish His kingdom purpose. Every authority has its specific jurisdiction. Each believer receives the necessary authority and must use it within the scope of their calling. That is why we need to be sure of our particular calling, as I mentioned earlier.

A mother who stays at home but is called to intercessory prayer may have more spiritual jurisdiction than a local leader of a church. You won't know who holds the key of authority to certain regions and over nations. Most of the time they are not well known or popular. They are hidden in the natural, but they are well known in the spirit.

Now the simple question comes: what if you are a person who is faithfully working in an office and not this super-special person with all these unique talents. How will you exercise your kingdom authority? There are all kinds of ways God could use you. Begin simply by listening to Him and doing the things He guides you to do. You don't have to be super-special in anything to accomplish the goals Jesus has set for you. He has used ordinary people to begin schools, teach children, and develop products—all kinds of things. Whether what you do affects many people or a small number does not matter. Trusting Jesus and obeying Him is what matters: Reaching your full potential and accomplishing your God-given mission on earth. We are only expected to use what He has given us, with no concern about what He has not, because He has equipped us for the tasks at hand. May all we do honor and please Jesus in the end.

I encourage you to pray the Lord's Prayer whenever you can. If you are part of an ekklesia, when you come together, pray this prayer as a group. I have paraphrased the prayer for you below. You are free to personalize it as the Holy Spirit leads.

Our Father in heaven, hallowed be Your name. Let Your name be made holy in our nation, in my family, and in the whole earth.

Thank You for giving us Your kingdom. Help us to administer it effectively on earth. Teach us how to tap into Your kingdom resources to solve problems on this earth.

Let Your kingdom rule and dominion come into my life, family, and nation.

Let Your kingdom government, family, economy, culture, education, and health come to this earth, in my life, nation, and family. Let Your will be done on earth as it is in heaven. Give us this day our daily, physical, financial, spiritual, and emotional bread (ideas, solutions, favor, wisdom, grace, connections).
And forgive us our debts,
As we forgive our debtors.

(If there is anyone you need to forgive, say their name and release forgiveness from your heart.)
And do not lead us into temptation,
But deliver us from the evil one and his works.

Thank You for delivering us from evil, curses, offenses, jealousy, strife, sickness, ignorance, fear, deception, lies, debt, lack, and poverty.
For Yours is the kingdom and the power and the glory forever. Amen.

More Books & Resources

DISCIPLING NATIONS SERIES

Kingdom Mandate (for any donation)
Discovering the Lost Kingdom (Volume 1) $14.00
Purpose, Calling, and Gifts (Volume 2) $15.00
God's Original Design (Volume 3) $20.00
Seeing, Entering, and Manifesting the Kingdom of God (Volume 4)$20.00
The Ekklesia (Volume 5) $30.00
The Gospel of the Kingdom (Volume 6) $20.00
Power and Authority of the Church (Volume 7) $15.00
Kingdom Family (Volume 8) $15.00
The Birthing of a Kingdom Nation (Volume 9) $20.00
What Happened to God? (Volume 10) $20.00
7 Dimensions and Operations of the Kingdom of God (Volume 11) $15.00
Kingdom Economy (Volume 12) $15.00
Kingdom Government (Volume 13) $15.00
Releasing Kings and Queens into God's Original Intent (Volume 14) $10.00
Kingdom Secrets to Restoring Nations Back to God (Volume 15) $20.00
Keys to Fulfilling Your Kingdom Assignment (Volume 16) $20.00

KINGDOM LIVING SERIES

The Three Most Important Decisions of Your Life $15.00
Recognizing God's Timing for Your Life $12.00
Overcoming the Spirit of Poverty $10.00
Seven Kinds of Believers $10.00
7 Dimensions of God's Glory $5.00
7 Dimensions of God's Grace $10.00
7 Kinds of Faith $8.00

HEALING OF THE NATIONS SERIES

Principles of Self Governance $20.00

KINGDOM BOOKS FOR KIDS

Genesis 126 Three Volume Book set for boys $25.00
Genesis 126 Three Volume Book set for girls $25.00

Genesis 126 Coloring Books for Boys $10.00
Genesis 126 Coloring Books for Girls $10.00

GENESIS 126 TEACHER'S MANUAL

Level 1 6-8 years $15.00
Level 2 8-10 years $15.00
Level 3 10-12 years $15.00

TO PLACE AN ORDER:

www.TheKingdomNetwork.org
Phone: 1-800-558-5020
Email: info@TheKingdomNetwork.org

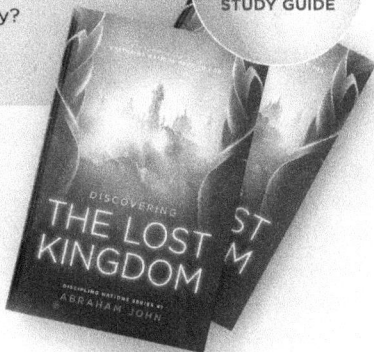

Welcome to

KINGDOM DELIVERANCE

— WORKSHOP —

Are you tired of waiting and looking for breakthroughs? Kingdom of God has the answer.

This kingdom deconstruct workshop is divided into EIGHT major categories which deal with the seven major areas of our life. Each one is connected to the next, and so if one of these areas dysfunctions, it will affect all other areas of your life.

1. Relationship with the Father
2. Spiritual Healing
3. Emotional Healing
4. Purpose and Calling
5. Mastering Gifts and Skills
6. Finances—Learning to Live in Kingdom Economy
7. Healing Relationships
8. Physical Health

Take action now. Order all 8 workshop manuals today !

Thank you so much for taking the courses from The Kingdom University.
Taking a course is only the first step. We are pleased to present you with the next step—that of going through the process to get rid of all the extra weights that have been slowing and hindering you from fully living out your kingdom assignment.

Call 1 800 558 5020   www.TheKingdomNetwork.org

www.ingramcontent.com/pod-product-compliance
Lightning Source LLC
Chambersburg PA
CBHW062129020426
42335CB00013B/1150